...Carl-Auer

The Organisation
of Self-Organisation

Fritz B. Simon/C/O/N/E/C/T/A-Authorgroup

Foundations of Systemic Management

Translated by Sally Hofmeister

2004

Published by Carl-Auer Verlag: **www.carl-auer.com**
Please order our catalogue:

Carl-Auer Verlag
Weberstrasse 2
69120 Heidelberg
Germany

Cover: WSP Design, Heidelberg
Printed in The Netherlands
Printed by Koninklijke Wöhrmann B. V., Zutphen

ISBN 3-89670-447-8

Title of the original edition:
„Radikale Marktwirtschaft"
© 2001 by Carl-Auer-Systeme, Heidelberg

Bibliographic information published by Die Deutschen Bibliothek
Die Deutsche Bibliothek lists this publication
in the Deutsche Nationalbibliografie; detailed bibliographic
data is available in the Internet at http://dnb.ddb.de.

Contents

1. Inctroduction ... 7

Management stories, theories and recipes ... 7
The systemic and the radical market economy model ... 11

2. Philsosophy ... 14

The Manager and his Horse – Reining in living systems ... 14
The influence of the observer – Harder and softer reality ... 17
The construction of reality – Distinguishing and naming ... 20
Predictability – Trivial and nontrivial machines ... 23
Creation without a creator – Self-organisation and evolution ... 28
Constancy and change ... 30
The external perspective – The employee as environment
    of the enterprise ... 31
The inner perspective – The enterprise as an individual's
    environment ... 35
The integration of outer and inner perspective – Behaviour as a
    commodity ... 37
Recipes ... 45

3. Organisation ... 46

The Housewife and the artist – Creating, maintaining and
    disintegrating order ... 46
Teamwork – Division of labour and cooperation ... 53
The lucky-dip effect – The behaviour of people as entities
    and its rating ... 60
The evolution of organisational patterns – An experiment ... 66
Recipes ... 69

4. Performance ... 71

The efficacy of "efficiency" ... 71
Paradox – Performance in a corporate planned economy ... 74
The black market – The self-organisation of unplanned
    control structures ... 77
Recipes ... 84

5

5. Leadership ... 85

Generals without soldiers – The peculiar military metaphors
of management ... 85
Power – Who wants what from whom? ... 90
Complexity – The manager's many markets ... 93
Magic – How language creates reality ... 95
Witchcraft – The manager, inside and outside at the same time ... 98
Mother and executioner – The personnel division as trivialiser ... 102
Recipes ... 106

6. Planning ... 108

Weathermen and rainmakers – The soft reality of the economy ... 108
From "strategic planning" to "evolutionary planning" ... 110
The positive power of "negative" thinking – The conditions
of dying and the limits of survival ... 116
A good answer, but what is the question? – Enterprise, product
and buyer ... 117
The life cycle of products ... 122
Monopoly versus optimal market shares ... 124
Hiking in the mountains – Between planning and improvisation ... 126
Recipes ... 129

7. Culture ... 131

Dangerous and other patterns ... 131
The Organisation of Balance ... 136
The madly chaotic and the psychosomatically ordered pattern ... 139
Establishing culture ... 145
Recipes ... 148

8. Sex Roles ... 150

Small differences, big differences ... 150
Sex roles ... 153
Management as an all-male club ... 154
The Family as fitness centre ... 157
Recipes ... 159

9. Learning ... 161

The storage metaphor ... 162
Knowledge and learning as principles of explanation ... 163
Selecting behaviour ... 164
Who adapts to whom? ... 165
Principles ... 166
The prevention of learning ... 167
Recipes ... 169

10. Postscript – about this book ... 172
About the Authors ... 174

1. Introduction

"A man wanted to know about mind, not in nature, but in his private,
large computer. He asked it (no doubt in his best Fortran),
"Do you compute that you will ever think like a human being?"
The machine then set to work to analyse its own computational habits.
Finally, the machine printed its answer on a piece of paper,
as such machines do. The man ran to get the answer and found,
neatly typed, the words: That reminds me of a story."
Gregory Bateson[1]

"Theories pass away. The frog stays."
Jean Rostand[2]

"It may be helpful at this stage to realise that the primary form
of mathematical communication is not description, but injunction.
In this respect it is comparable with practical art forms like cookery,
in which the taste of a cake, although literally indescribable,
can be conveyed to a reader in the form of a set of injunctions
called a recipe."
George Spencer-Brown[3]

MANAGEMENT STORIES, THEORIES AND RECIPES

If we study the deluge of books and magazines on the subject of management, we can, roughly classified, identify three different types of publications:

1   G. Bateson (1979): Mind and Nature: A Necessary Unity. New York (Dutton), Bantom Edition 1980, p. 14.
2   J. Rostand (1959): Carnet d'un biologiste. Paris (Stock).
3   G. Spencer-Brown (1969): Laws of Form. New York (Dutton) 1977, p. 77.

a) Recipe books in which management know-how is imparted.

These are constructed on the pattern of a cookery book: If such and such is the case, then you take this and do that … They are intended for practical people with both feet on the ground who ask themselves daily: What is to be done? They have to make decisions with possible far-reaching consequences for themselves, their colleagues, their businesses, their families and a great number of other people. Such books or magazines offer nicely photographed menu suggestions for someone who has to get some kind of meal on the table every day and fill hungry mouths. They usually also provide a list of the necessary ingredients and instructions for preparation.

All in all, recipes and recipe books can be very useful and practical as they tell the reader how to achieve certain goals (for example "peak performance") (= prescriptive rules). Adhering to cooking recipes certainly complies with our search for simplification and certainty; however, the danger of such recipe collections lies in the fact that they tempt us to look for problem solutions on a purely "technical" level without adequate analysis. This can easily lead to essential connections being lost to view, which can mean the best intentions leading to the worst results. Besides: The amount of ingredients for a cake or a roast are clear, as are the pertinent instructions. Working out a marketing strategy is much more complicated.

b) The second type of publication, to be found not only in university libraries and institutes, concerns itself with theories. In this case what happens while cooking – to keep to the same metaphor – is described and explained from the position of the external observer.

Someone who writes up theories is generally free from any pressure to make decisions: he does not have to deal with conflicts about whose favourite meal to cook and which ingredients he should use for which meal in which quantities. As he is neither obliged to consume the product of this more or less great culinary art himself, nor to sell it or pour it down anyone else's throat, he can, from the perspective of an uninvolved spectator, coolly establish that it generally has fatal consequences for the economic survival of a restaurant when the chef de cuisine continuously mistakes salt for sugar.

The use of these scientific findings exists first and foremost in the fact that they describe correlations that can be observed regularly (= descriptive rules). Someone in real everyday life then has to make his own choice as to which of these findings could be of use to him. For it is by no means certain that the person publishing his observations and explanations has ever cooked anything himself or had to eat it. For this reason it is also by no means certain that the factors and variables described and combined by scientists and theorists have any meaning for the daily business of doers.

c) And then there are all the stories that are told: Once upon a time there was a little Italian boy in America who had always wanted to become a pizza baker and ended up as the successful boss of an automobile company.

From the vantage point of cultural history such stories constitute a very old form of literature. They have been told for thousands of years. In the beginning, however, it was by no means a question of conquering markets, but rather of conquering Troy. Apart from that, though, the pattern is quite similar: The heroes, Odysseus and Achilles, members of the executive board of a joint venture between various middle-class enterprises, had not only to struggle against the King of Troy and his sons, the directors of a competitive family business in Asia Minor, but also with leadership problems; with the difficulty of motivating their employees in a battle lasting ten years, for example. In addition they had to cope with all the complications ensuing from the mainly unforeseeable interventions of the members of the board of directors on some Olympus or other, who were sometimes on bad terms and at others entangled in erotic adventures.

The success of such myths, epic tales and autobiographies over the ages might well be due to the fact that here internal and external observational perspectives are connected. Spellbound, the listener or reader follows the words of the storyteller, who knows the whole story from beginning to end and seems to report its ups and downs with the detached view of a spectator. From this perspective it is clear why everything had to happen the way it did. The inevitability of the dramatic production, the clandestine rules of these dramas, which are not consciously known to the persons currently entangled in the action of the plot and remain in the dark, become transparent. The readers can identify with the leading actors, their thoughts and emotions. What would I have done in a comparable situation? Which of the hero's or heroine's recipes for success can I earmark for my own behavioural repertoire? What sweeping conclusions can I infer from this and similar stories, the fates and biographies of the successful men and women of this world, executives, for example?

People think in stories[4], thus these stories are particularly suitable for presenting complex correlations. The advantage over a mere collection of recipes or theories is obvious: Stories connect prescriptive and descriptive rules. The individual actors adhere to certain prescriptive rules with their recipes for success or failure and their values, and thereby proceed from the tacit presumption of certain descriptive rules: their world view, their convictions and ideas on how life, the economy, people etc. function in "reality". The disadvantage of these stories is that they are often very ambiguous and leave all too much scope for interpretation. They report individual cases, and it is doubtful whether and how these exemplary experiences can be generalised.

The intention of this book is to look for a few answers to these questions. To this end all three outlined methods of description, insight and presentation are connected: stories are told, analyses and theoretical reflections made and finally recipes for the everyday life of managers or employers distilled from the whole. The result is a collection of management rules or rather rules for management games.

The use of the term "game" may perhaps have a somewhat disturbing effect in this context. But on closer observation we find that games and stories are related. The number of rules that can be used to describe a certain game (football, chess, bridge, market economy, planned economy and all the others) provides, as it were, the blueprint, the dramatic pattern out of which all the individual stories can be constructed, or vice versa: these characteristic rules can be filtered out of the many stories. Stories are always merely the report of single games or players ("How I once owned Boardwalk, Park Avenue, four

---

4   See W. Schapp (1953): In Geschichten verstrickt. Leer (Rautenberg) 1959.
See also G. Bateson (1979): Mind and Nature. A Necessary Unity. New York (Dutton).

railroads and 27 hotels in Monopoly..." or "When I once took over the XY company / became market leader in this or that line of business / became a successful ...").

Success or failure in life always depends on the knowledge of which game one is playing. A successful hand-ball player who unerringly scores goals will fail miserably if all the other players on the field are playing football. And a celebrated opera singer will receive little applause if the audience has come to listen to a pop concert.

Which games are played where and when, and what are the rules? Recipes for success (or failure) cannot be applied consciously until these questions have been answered. Sometimes one can then – if it seems reasonable – even find recipes for changing these rules.

THE SYSTEMIC AND THE RADICAL MARKET ECONOMY MODEL

The manager as strategist, the corporate boardroom as the general's mound, the company as an army with headquarters and line ...

War is only one of the metaphors governing our ideas of business management and market economy. The language used to depict economic life is full of such open and hidden metaphors. The popularity of comparisons from warfare and biology is certainly not coincidental. Economy and society as a whole, sometimes its subsystems, too (enterprises, markets, whole national economies or their elements), are often compared to living organisms, plants or even human individuals: a flourishing business, the growth of the economy, the head of the company, the parent company, galloping inflation, a healthy firm, the administrative organs, the invisible hand that controls everything. War then seems merely the continuation of biology with different means, the Darwinian struggle for survival seems to be a logical consequence.

This book attempts to show that the reversal of these metaphors can also be useful, perhaps even more useful. This allows the observation of all individual and social patterns of behaviour pertinent to economic life from an economic perspective: in this case national economies are not only compared to organisms, but also organisms to national economies, the gross individual product replaces the gross national product, all interaction between human beings, whether private or business, can then be understood as a form of market economy.

11

Placing familiar metaphors on their heads like this seems at first very radical, of course, and is in danger of being condemned from the outset as reactionary, banal or even immoral. We are used to dividing the world and our lives into two strictly separate areas: on the one hand our economic and working life in which economic considerations are in the foreground, and on the other our private life: love, family, children, friends. In the first area we try to behave rationally, for reason (ostensibly) determines economic success and failure. In the second area emotion is the ruler and economic considerations and logic – so widespread conviction would have it – have no business here; at least they often seem difficult to find. The radical market economy viewpoint suggested here cancels the often illusionary separation between economy and emotion and frequently does not even halt before the holy realm of emotional interpersonal relationships; it offers us the chance to develop a model that clarifies the clandestine reason and economy of individual, group and organisational behaviour.

The theoretical foundation for this model ensues from recent developments in systems and evolution theory, the concepts of the theory of cognition of so-called "radical constructivism" and "second order cybernetics". Where necessary, these theoretical basics will be briefly outlined. First of all, however, the basic hypothesis of the "radical market economy"[5] model should be set out:

Action = transaction. That means someone who carries out an action is always carrying out a transaction. Or, to put it another way: Human behaviour can always be seen as a commodity that can be evaluated and exchanged.

5   The term "radical market economy" should be understood as a metaphor; it is intended to refer to the theoretical relationship to "radical constructivism". In view of the correct use of language it would, of course, have been better policy to speak of "radical economy". But not only feeling for language rebels against this terminological monster, but it could also result in confusion with the theoretical school of "radical economics" which arose in the USA in the second half of the sixties; see the magazine *The Review of Radical Economics* founded in 1969 or also the summary by M. Bronfenbrenner (1979): Radical Economics in America. *Journal of Economic Literature* 3, 747 ff.

More important, it seems to us, is the baffling similarity with Gary S. Becker's approach, who tries in general to explain human behaviour economically. In 1992 he received the Nobel prize for his work; see G. S. Becker: The Economic Explanation to Human Behaviour. University of Chicago Press, 1978.

This simple rule has far-reaching consequences: Life appears to be an exchange, a coalescence between supply and demand in accordance with certain behaviours and actions. A living being has to prove the worth of his modes of behaviour on many very different markets and in opposition to a great number of fellow competitors. Economic life is only one of these.

Ten basic hypotheses of the
radical market economy model

1. Action = transaction.

2. The market for behavior is an
exchange market.

3. Every individual evaluates the behavior
(= commodity) produced by himself
or others according to his own system
of values.

4. Everyone behaves always and everywhere
in an economically rational way.

5. Everyone keeps a give-and-take account
for all partners in interaction (his own
and that of the other) in his own private,
non-convertible currency.

6. Concrete patterns of interaction arise in
compliance with the individual systems of
values of those concerned and their
accounting methods.

7. "Personality", "character" and "personal
identity" can also be explained as a
function of the differences between
individual accounting methods.

8. People can also market themselves.

9. A commodity (= ware) is only something
that one is aware of.

10. There is no objective standard of
evaluation for the value of behavior.

Fig. 1

2. Philsosophy

> "The French maintain that camels are dumb,
> cruel and vindictive animals who must be forced
> to obey by means of shouting and beatings (…)
> All year round the French treated all camels the same way
> without understanding that the animals can be
> irritable and dangerous during the rutting season,
> particularly when the heat increased
> with the easterly winds. For this reason
> the French never became good riders in the desert,
> and that is why they never succeeded in ruling
> the Tuareg, but were conquered by them again and
> again during the years of fighting and feuds,
> although they were superior in number and better armed."
>
> Alberto Vazques-Figueroa[1]

> "The unit of survival – either in ethics or in evolution –
> is not the organism or the species but the largest system or 'power'
> within which the creature lives.
> If the creature destroys its environment, it destroys itself."
>
> Gregory Bateson[2]

THE MANAGER AND HIS HORSE –
REINING IN LIVING SYSTEMS

The close relationship between the terms manager and manège (fr.:
circus ring) reminds us that the art of management lies in the reining

---

1 A. Vazques-Figueroa (1981): Tuareg. Munich (Goldmann) 1990, p. 16.
2 G. Bateson (1971): The Cybernetics of "Self". In: Steps to an Ecology of Mind.
New York (Ballantine) 1983, p. 332.

14

in and use of living systems, first of all that of horses: Managing originally meant to train, ride and control a horse[3]. In general we can rely
on the wisdom of the knowledge stored in our language. When terms
are used in a figurative sense this occurs because they fit somehow,
that is they denote something common: the rider and his horse – the
manager and his business (his department/his team etc.).

This metaphor outlines the whole problem confronting a manager: he tries to keep a tight rein on a living system, guide it and
determine its behaviour, its gait and its pace. He sits firmly in the
saddle (when someone has helped him on), holds onto the reins,
spurs it on and occasionally uses the persuasive power of stick and
carrot. A circus artiste who turns somersaults on her horse's back
manages her horse without reins; it knows her and knows what she
wants. There are good and bad riders, and one finds patient horses
who bear (in both senses of the word) even the clumsiest riders, thor-
oughbred stallions hard to control next to cold-blooded brewery
carthorses. One rider is capable of taming wild horses, the next passes
horse-jumping competitions with style, the third is unbeatable in
horse-racing; but you also find knackers who manage to destroy any
horse.

Ideally horse and rider are a unit, their actions are coordinated,
their courses and careers are connected, and together they reach their
goal: and it is not always the rider's. If they get into rough, dangerous terrain they have to rely on each other. Sometimes they are even
a survival unit when the existence of one depends on the behaviour
of the other in a hostile environment.

The relationship between the two is complicated: As organisms
they are principally in a position to survive independently. Both have
a large scope of action, and diverse behavioural options are open to
them as individuals. They do not have to cooperate, but they do ...
The economic explanation: They decide to do it because it's a good
deal for both.

The horse-and-rider model is useful to characterise the possibilities and necessities that limit the art of management in two ways:

---

3   Derived from the Italian maneggiare, see Latin *manus:* hand; see C. T. Onions
(1985): The Oxford Dictionary of English Etymology. London (Oxford University
Press) p. 550.

Firstly, the manager has to deal with people as living systems – colleagues, subordinates and superiors, consumers, customers and suppliers etc.; secondly firms as a whole, whether his own or that of his fellow competitors, have certain characteristics comparable to those of living beings: they are self-organising systems which go through a process of evolution in interaction with their environment in which they and their environment change conjointly or stabilise each other.

Let's stretch the (of course inappropriate) comparison between the demands on managers and riders a little more and come to the philosophical epistemological question: What must one know or be capable of, in order to stay in the saddle successfully and reach the goal safe and sound and with a healthy horse? What information is useful, what is rather confusing? It is well known that too much knowledge makes one dumb. You probably don't need any knowledge of the biochemical processes of the animal's digestion, whereas it is important to have some idea of what it likes to eat, what is good for it and how it reacts to constipation. Theories on its metabolism are of no direct use. You need knowledge from which practical instructions can be deduced: How does the horse or camel react to the behaviour of its rider? Does the living system you are dealing with at the moment react in the same way as those you have already experienced? Can you always treat it according to the same recipes? Or sometimes like this and another time like that? Can we, with impunity, deduct from certain similarities between these systems that everything is similar? Must we treat camels differently to horses? And is this experiential knowledge we have acquired in the course of our lives valid always and everywhere – in the desert and in the rutting season as well as in the oasis or in times of sexual disinterest (the camel's, of course)?

Learning management is, of course, a little more complicated than learning to ride a horse or a camel. For it is often not so obvious where the rider stops and the animal begins. Is not the behaviour of the manager or even the manager as a whole part of the company he wants to ride? The answer to this question has a number of very practical consequences for the everyday life of a manager.

THE INFLUENCE OF THE OBSERVER — HARDER AND SOFTER REALITY

Too much knowledge can be lethal: In old Wild West films we sometimes see scenes in which an unpleasant witness is shot in the back. But there are other examples for knowledge not only meaning power: The State Security Service of the former German Democratic Republic, whose task it was, among other things, to keep a watch on and control of the population, was not able to prevent demonstrations and revolution because it had too much information. It suffocated under a flood of data which could not be analysed and evaluated, so that no political consequences could be drawn from it.

We are more familiar with all the situations in which too little knowledge causes harm: When we get lost and lose our sense of orientation because we don't know the area and have no map to show us where we are; when we don't know the usual market price for a commodity and get cheated; when we don't know a production technique, don't speak a language etc. ... Ignorance means powerlessness. Only too easily this experience leads us to the dangerous reverse conclusion: the more knowledge the better. Good reason to take the maxim seriously "What the eye does not see, the heart does not grieve over" can be deducted from elementary considerations of epistemology.[4]

The world is tremendously complex, confusing and unfathomable, no less the world of economy. Everyone – not just the manager – needs to construe his own picture of reality, a kind of inner map, which enables him to act meaningfully. The value of all knowledge – scientific as well as everyday – depends on the purpose and goals for which it is needed. It is a question of using appropriate behaviour. To do this, the complexity of the world has to be reduced and a selection made from the possible knowledge which gives us orientation. And it is not only a question of the adequate quantity of information, but also of its quality. Not truth, but usefulness is the standard by which it is measured.

Cognition, that is the development of an individual or collective world view, has among other things a biological effect: Success proves itself in the survival of organisms, failure in their death. However, this goal, securing survival, can be achieved with very different constructions of reality. They just have to fit somehow to the world

4 For details see F. B. Simon (1997): Die Kunst, nicht zu lernen. Und andere Paradoxien in Psychiatrie, Management, Politik ... Heidelberg (Carl-Auer).

in which they are used; that means – quite simply – it has to be possible to survive with the respective world view: Whosoever survives has adapted.[5] Many roads lead to Rome. There isn't just one right and true road to Rome that you can objectively know or not know. You can take many different roads, there are more than you would ever have thought possible.[6]

This formula allows the description of the basic positions of the epistemological and scientific theory of Radical Constructivism. They have been developed from the findings of developmental psychology and brain research, which show that everyone constructs his own distinctive picture of the world in interaction with his own living and inanimate environment.

The same objective physical events lead to different perceptions and world views in different observers, dependent on the conditions of their observations. Each person lives in his own reality, even if in many fields he agrees with his fellow men on a mutual view of reality called objective. The position of observation determines what is seen.

It is inevitably easiest for a number of people to agree on what is "real" where the influence of observation on what is being observed is smallest. In the first place this is valid for those areas in which a clear distinction between the observer and the object observed can be guaranteed. Engineers and mechanics are usually in the happy position of not being an element of the machine they are building or maintaining. They are dealing with an area of reality – like the so-called "hard sciences" – which is relatively "hard" and whose functioning is not, or only minimally, influenced by the fact that it is being observed.[7] No machine goes red and starts stuttering when it is called "stupid", no chemical falls into a crisis of self-esteem when the chemist doesn't like it, and no computer can be enticed to work faster by incentive trips.

It is quite different in the area dealt with by the so-called 'soft sciences' and by all those whose task it is to intervene in social sys-

---

5   See M. Eigen and R. Winkler (1975): Laws of the Game. How the Principles of Nature Govern Chance. Princeton, NJ (Princeton University Press) 1993.

6   See the essays on Radical Constructivism, in particular E. von Glasersfeld (1987): The Construction of Knowledge. Contributions to Conceptual Semantics. Seaside, CA. (Intersystems Publications).

7   Since Heisenberg's insight that in microphysics phenomena are changed by their observation, we know that this is no longer quite true. See W. Heisenberg (1959): Physik und Philosophie. Berlin (Ullstein) 1963.

tems, for example states, markets, enterprises, families etc. In this area of reality the division between subject and object, so successful in natural science, is often problematical, sometimes even absolutely inadequate. Top executives, politicians and family members contribute to maintaining or changing the social systems they are observing; and the very fact of their observation is a decisive factor that has an effect. Social reality, the reality of human action and economy, is relatively "soft", that is, changeable by observation:[8] Someone who is described as able, competent and effective gets on in the world, someone known as a loser can "objectively"(?) be as good as he wants, he will never succeed in life. Public opinion and mood, fashion and image determine which commodities will sell and which become stickers. In this soft area of reality any attempt to proceed with the calculating objectivity of the natural scientist or engineer is inevitably doomed to failure.

A good reason to occupy oneself a little with epistemology and to direct one's attention to the mechanisms with the help of which we as humans construct our individual and collective reality.

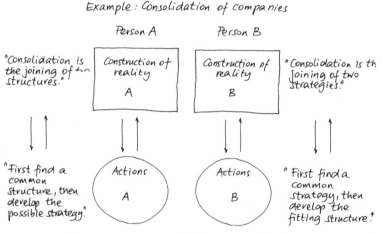

Example : Consolidation of companies

Fig. 2

---

8 See the more exact differentiation between "softer" and "harder" reality in F. B. Simon (1990): My Psychosis, my Bicycle and I. The Self-Organisation of Madness. Northvale, NJ (Jason Aronson) 1996.

THE CONSTRUCTION OF REALITY —
DISTINGUISHING AND NAMING

The misunderstanding that information is something objective that can be collected like stamps is widespread. Information is neither a thing that can be packed into a brief-case, nor some kind of picture or data that can be kept in a photo album, a computer or cerebrum. Whether any kind of phenomena becomes information for an observer depends mainly on the person himself. Anyone who has difficulty understanding the refinements of the economy will have difficulty understanding the market-quotations in the financial newspaper, not just today, but every day and for ever more. On the other hand, an expert in the scene will read trends in the daily price oscillations, get stomach-ache or emit shouts of jubilation, make decisions to buy and sell. This information is not objective, though. Every reader derives different information from the same phenomenon, the printer's ink on the paper. One reads the daily differences in market dynamics, for others the spate of numbers allows no recognition of any differences. The conditions of the observer, or rather of observation, determine what information value certain phenomena have for him.

The anthropologist Gregory Bateson defines "information" as "any difference that makes a difference."[9] What is information (makes a difference) for one person is not (makes no difference) for the other. We do not pick up our view of the world passively the way paper is printed, but actively, more like a video camera: If it is not switched on, it cannot work and produces no pictures; the refinement of the pictures not only depends on the depicted objects, but on the camera's acuity of image; and the colour saturation transformed into information by a colour film makes no difference for a black and white film. There is no clear-cut cause-and-effect relationship between external reality and the picture of it, no inevitable similarity; the observer's structures always determine what he observes, or rather what he can observe. Another banal example: When you walk through a city hungry, you often only see restaurants, when you walk

9 G. Bateson (1979): Mind and Nature: A Necessary Unity. New York (Dutton), Bantom Edition 1980, p. 250.

the same way with a pleasantly satisfied feeling in your stomach you won't notice them at all. If you have just bought a certain model of car, for a while you will have the feeling that you practically only see this model on the road.

The English mathematician George Spencer-Brown proves that all logical structures, all forms of human thinking can be attributed to such distinctions.[10] He compares the process of differentiation with drawing a circle on a sheet of paper. With this procedure a boundary is drawn and an area inside the circle (= not outside) is separated from the space outside the circle (= not inside). Due to the biologically given mechanisms of our perception we are always drawing boundaries and subdividing continuous processes in discontinuous sections. We construct contrasting pairs or units that are limited by an environment.

The form of these units is mutually created by what is enclosed and excluded by this distinction, by what is on each side of the boundary.

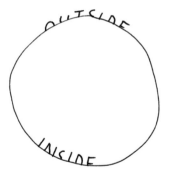

We draw a border between inside and outside by the process of perception.

Fig. 3

Both sides of such distinctions, the constructed unit and its environment, can be labelled, that is attributed a name, a concept, a sign or a value. This brings the ability of human beings to handle signs and

10 G. Spencer-Brown (1969): Laws of Form. New York (Dutton) 1979.

symbols – i. e. labels – into play, for language plays a decisive role in creating people's world views. With the help of language we can not only exchange ideas on the directly observed world, but also on the area of our reality which is not accessible to direct perception. The development of our opinions on abstract principles and rules of the game, on moral and ethical values, feelings and reason, right and wrong, good and bad, strong and weak are bound to language, its structure and use. We are dealing here with a relatively soft area of reality. Concepts change their meaning in the course of time, and different people use the same concepts with varying meanings. If we do not realise that the same objective phenomena do not lead to the same labels (allocation of terms, names, signs or values) we are in danger of confusing the map with the landscape, traffic signs with traffic regulations, the menu with the meal, a Business School certificate with the ability to manage a company.

If we want to know the concrete meaning of these signs, we have to examine which meanings the person using them (an individual, a culture or subculture etc.) allocates to the two sides of the distinction – inside and outside the circle. It must be explicitly emphasised that the meaning of signs is always determined by both sides of the distinction, since this is not obvious from our everyday use of language and sign systems. For reasons of economy, it is usually only the inside of the distinction that is named, that is the qualities and distinctive features of things, systems, structures, individuals and atoms, and not the "obvious" features of their environment – the outside of the distinction. It is only when this environment, on which we base our presumptions as a matter of course, is not guaranteed that it becomes clear that the forms and features of the objects we observe are an effect of the interplay of both sides of the distinction, of inside and outside: A human being is only a human being as long as there is enough oxygen in his environment to allow him to maintain his organic structure. The meaning of the term "human being" can thus include a lot more than just the qualities of an organism.

For practice, let us take two simple examples: the concepts "Rome", to which, as we know, many roads lead, and "survival" as one goal of knowledge. Someone to whom Rome merely means eating pizza can be satisfied by finding the way to the Italian restaurant on the corner. Someone who wants to meet the Pope can also safely stay at home, since at sometime or another he passes through everywhere; and someone who wants to see St. Peter's will enjoy himself immensely by inviting himself round to his neighbour's to look at his slides. What Rome means for a person becomes clear when you ask him two questions: (1) How many things can you imagine not being in Rome, and yet Rome still being Rome (i. e. what must definitely be within the circle)? And: (2) What makes you realise that it is not Rome (i. e. what must definitely be outside the circle)? Would Rome still be Rome if the Pope moved to Avignon? Would Rome still be Rome if the Walt Disney Corporation bought up St. Peter's and transplanted it to Florida as an amusement park? Or would it then be Florida? If all the inhabitants lived in igloos could this settlement still be Rome? Only when it is positively and absolutely clear what elements comprise this unit "Rome" – the city with all its museums, churches, the Pope, the pizzerias, the Colosseum, Castel Sant'Angelo, the love affair twenty years ago and so on – only then can we infer what the goal of someone's trip to Rome really is.

The same applies for the concept and value of "survival". Is it survival when you lose your reputable job, your partner leaves you, your child dies, your company goes bankrupt, your neighbours no longer greet you, your statements don't tally, you make losses, the newspapers publish libellous articles etc.? Is it still life when you are in a coma hitched up to machines that maintain the most important biological functions? What distinguishes life from non-life?

PREDICTABILITY –
TRIVIAL AND NONTRIVIAL MACHINES

How many psychologists do you need to screw in a light bulb? The answer is easy: In principle just one! But: The light bulb must really want to be put in!

This old psychologist joke can be applied to the situation of the manager: his task has a target, but he cannot just turn something in order to fulfil it successfully. Contrary to an electrician or a mechanic, he is not dealing with inanimate objects that obey the laws of nature and can be governed provided he knows these laws. Far more so than any psychologist, the manager must do justice to the complexity of a dynamic and changing living world. He is entangled in an inscrutable network of interaction, has to calculate with unpredictable quantities, markets and powers. And he is dealing with people who sometimes – contrary to light bulbs – show their brilliant beam and illuminating power at the very time when they lose control (are no longer in the light socket) – but not always!

In our Western world the most wide-spread and generally very successfully practiced pattern of governing the complexity of the world lies in our cause-and-effect thinking. We see ourselves as external observers, the object to be examined as a "black box" whose inner life is unknown. Someone who finds such a box while turning out the loft and, inspired with scientific curiosity, wants to find out how it works, can subject it to a systematic scientific examination. Let us assume that the inquisitive explorer of the box is presented with the following picture: On the outside of the box there are four different buttons and four different lights. The buttons are coloured; one is red, one green, one yellow and one blue. The light bulbs are also coloured: red, green, yellow and blue. Our explorer can now compile a catalogue of input-output relations: For example, when he presses the red button, the red light always lights up, when he presses the yellow button, the yellow one and when he presses the green button the green light bulb shines, and when he presses the blue button, the blue one. In the case taken as an example his laboratory record might look like this:

Color of button	Color of lamp
red	red
yellow	yellow
green	green
blue	blue

Fig. 4

So this black box has a relatively straightforward structure, its repertoire of behaviour is very simple. It can be described by sentences

such as: "Whenever I press the red button, the red bulb lights up."
There seems to be some kind of cause-and-effect relationship between
pressing the button and the bulb lighting up. It is self-evident that
prescriptive rules, that is, instructions for action, can be derived from
such descriptive rules: "If you want the green lamp to light up just
press the green button!"

This kind of box functions on the principles of the so-called
"trivial machine"[11]. We do not need to know anything about its inner
state, we can manage it if we know the relation between input and
output. We can operate and use most of the technical appliances confronting us daily because they (fortunately) work on this principle:
We do not need to know anything about the mechanisms inside an
internal combustion engine in order to drive our cars, and we need
know nothing about transistors and picture tubes in order to turn on
our television sets. The inner life of all these useful appliances makes
no difference to us because it remains constant and thus its operation is predictable. It is part of a hard reality that is not changed by
examining it. Only when such a machine is defective must a specialist for its innards be called to restore its triviality, that is, its predictability.

The situation is completely different in the case of so-called "nontrivial machines". Let us assume we are again dealing with a black
box with exactly the same exterior as the first box: On the outside are
four coloured buttons and four coloured bulbs. The only difference:
The machine has two different inner states: It can be "willing" or
"unwilling", or to put it differently it can be in state A or B, in a good
or a bad mood. The name we choose for these two states is arbitrary,
so let us stick to "good" or "bad mood".

What our machine's mood is like at a certain time depends – quite
humanely – on what its mood was like before. Every operation of the
button ought to have an effect on its mood and either alter or confirm it. The curious behaviour of such a moody machine is exempli-
fied in the two tables. The middle columns show respectively whether
and how the inner state of the machine changes when the button is

11 See H. von Foerster (1988): Abbau und Aufbau. In: F. B. Simon (1988): Lebende
Systeme. Berlin/Heidelberg/New York (Springer), p. 19–33.

pressed (+ = mood remains or becomes good, - = mood remains or becomes bad). If the mood remains unchanged, the relation between button and bulb can be read from the same table, but if the machine's mood changes its reaction to the next push of the button can be read from the other table:

Machine's reaction when in a good mood (+)			Machine's reaction when in a bad mood (−)		
Color of button	Color of bulb	Mood becomes	Color of button	Color of bulb	Mood becomes
red	red	+	red	green	+
yellow	yellow	−	yellow	blue	+
green	green	+	green	yellow	−
blue	blue	−	blue	red	−

Fig. 5

If our fictitious explorer who cannot look at the inside of this machine tries to deduce its structure from the input-output relationships, he would likely be driven to the brink of despair. At first he has no dark foreboding: As in the case of the first machine he enters red and gets red back and for yellow he gets yellow back. But now the object's treacherousness is revealed: Pressing the yellow button completely spoilt the machine's mood (-) and has its effect when the next button is pressed. If the input is now green, the yellow bulb lights up again. "Apparently this machine makes mistakes," our researcher thinks. But, contrary to his expectations, when the blue button is pressed, the red light appears. Scientifically well-trained, he decides to repeat the experiment. He starts again with red, and this time he gets green, for yellow he gets yellow, for green yellow and for blue red. Increasingly confused, he decides to press each button several times in succession: For red he first gets green, then red, red, red, only red. He now tries the yellow button and the reaction is: Yellow, blue, yellow, blue … He will be occupied for a long time trying out all possibilities. For only two input and output values there are 2^{16}, that is 65,536 possible combinations.

Thus even in such a simple case it takes a lot of perseverance to try out all the various possibilities. This is altogether impossible if the number of possible input and output values increases. If there are only eight values, the number of possible machines increases to $10^{969685486}$, a number that renders the analysis of such a machine incalculable from steer lack of time. There are simply too many possibilities for all of them to be tried out.

The nontrivial machine envisaged here is, of course, a very good-natured specimen of its species. Its complexity simply cannot be compared to that of a horse, camel, or even of a person or an enterprise, or of the market with all their various moods. Their complexity is higher by several dimensions. For their inner life can not only change between various given states, but also create quite new states. The very attempt to analyse these can cause them to alter their structure. Market research can change the market, psychoanalysis the psyche – typical examples of softer reality.

The application of straightforward cause-effect thinking is hardly useful for dealing with such complex systems. The only possibility of retrieving a little of the world's lost predictability lies in the best possible modelling of the inner structures of the respective system, that is, the respective nontrivial machine. It is imperative then to make the best possible assumptions of the inner structures of a system (person, enterprise). The better a manager can try to understand or sympathise with an employee, for example, the easier it will be for him to assess his/her reaction to his management behaviour.

The simple picture of straightforward causality, in which little causes have only little effects and similar causes have similar effects, is not very useful. In all areas in which we are dealing with living beings (horses, camels, people, for example) or social systems (enterprises, markets, languages, cultures, religions etc., for example) its practicability is limited. All these complex systems shall (deviating from the normal use of language a little) be called "living systems", as they presuppose life and living beings. Their method of functioning differs fundamentally from that of trivial systems with which our simple cause-and-effect thinking can deal so successfully.

CREATION WITHOUT A CREATOR –
SELF-ORGANISATION AND EVOLUTION

Whether the world came into being because in the beginning was the word or the deed is a question disputed by biblical and other authors. But whichever answer to this issue may appeal to you, in both cases some kind of creator is tacitly assumed who made everything as it is; an observer who enjoys the weekend when his work is done and looks upon his work with more or less satisfaction. He spoke or acted, he made a decision and the world obeyed. Everything occurred as he contrived it: an omnipotent god as chief engineer. He is, as it were, the prime cause, the big banger. And if this creator shaped man in his own image, it then seems only logical that man often models himself on this model of an engineer. Let us turn the whole thing upside down (or right) and think it through the other way round: that it was man who created God in his own image und then used him to conceal the shortcomings of his own world view of cause and effect.

As we have probably all found out – happily or sorrowfully –, the world is not completely predictable: Man proposes, God disposes, and things never turn out the way one expects. The planning doesn't quite work somehow. So another, more powerful planner must have planned differently. If he exists, the presumptions about the world and its fundamental predictability need not be questioned.

The difficulties of a planned economy, this attempt to construct an economic system on the model of a trivial machine, the fact that wars always take a different course from the one planned by the strategists, and Murphy's law, according to which everything that can go wrong always will, are just a few examples for the limited possibilities of human planning and controlling.

The formation of structures in the course of evolutionary life processes differs above all in how the engineer idealises them. He defines what he needs a machine for, what behaviour it must be able to show, invents the necessary parts, thinks its operations through, has all the necessary elements made and tries hard to coordinate its actions. If he is successful, the machine will work as planned: On pressing the button it makes freshly brewed coffee, prints receipts or produces (in planned cooperation with other machines) whole cars.

Biological evolution, on the other hand, proceeds like a do-it-yourself man who keeps boxes full of screws, half-finished parts and wires without knowing whether and how he might find a use for them some time[12]. At some time in the future he then uses them for something not originally thought about; they are assembled to a new structure together with other parts and thus gain a function one would never have dreamt possible. But even the comparison with a do-it-yourself man is not quite apt, because this metaphor also presumes someone like a human who makes decisions and makes things with his hands. In the development of living systems, however, the decisions mostly make themselves: The elements of the junk box, shaken up by chance, get mixed up, some parts fit together, bow to an order and suddenly have a function. Living systems are self-organising; like traffic jams, they need no creator to plan them, they simply arise out of the combination of their elements ...

One of the fundamental prerequisites for the success of the engineer model is the distinction between the object to be put together and the person who puts it together. This usually works in putting machines together, but not in management. Even the comparison between horse and rider comes up against limiting factors here: Where does the rider end and the horse begin? The manager, or at least his behaviour, is an element of the enterprise (the horse) to be managed. This is why scientific insights are not often very useful for the manager as a practician: They, like other belief systems, are always formulated from the objectifying position of the external observer. Its utility is just as great or small as the smart-aleck commentary of a reporter up on the bleachers for a football player. At best, after the game, he can come to the obvious conclusions of such observations for the future, but in the current match he is always on his own. He needs a scheme according to which he can order and evaluate his perceptions, so that he is able – often under pressure – to make decisions.

To stretch the clumsy comparison yet again and then finish with it: The task of a manager is far more complicated than that of a rider. It is comparable to the task of a handicraft man who is crafting him-

---

12 See F. Jacob (1982): The Possible and the Actual. Seattle (University of Washington Press).

self into a piece of work on which a great number of others are working simultaneously.

CONSTANCY AND CHANGE

After being drilled for decades in schools and universities to see the world as a trivial machine, we risk our world view not fitting the world, our inner map not fitting the landscape. In our daily thoughts we usually tacitly presume that the world and all the objects we perceive in it stay as they are, unless someone or something changes them. Things seem to be static, a car does not usually budge unless someone starts the engine, changes gear and steps on the gas. If the car has a dent, it stays in the wing until a mechanic pounds it out. It seems natural that the status quo is maintained passively. Only change then needs explaining. Anyone who wishes to introduce change must, in accordance with such a world view, get active (make alterations, repair …). If nothing particular happens, so it seems, everything stays as it was.

The situation is the reverse in living, self-organising systems, however: Nothing remains passively as it is unless someone actively makes sure that it does. So if someone has a lump on his forehead, it disappears on its own after a while – in contrast to the wing of a car – unless the owner of the forehead makes sure it survives by regularly banging his head against a brick wall.[13] It is thus not the changing of structures that has to be explained, but rather their constancy. No organism receives its structure passively. It requires the functioning of a complicated metabolism, being supplied with food, excreting roughage and the products of metabolism, it needs to breathe in and out. Only so long as the activities which produce such living structures are maintained, does the living system remain a living system.

However, this is not only valid for living beings, but also for the systems that arise from their activities: A language no longer spoken dies out, an enterprise in which no-one works any more, that neither offers commodities nor services for sale on the market and has no income cannot survive. But it will also be destroyed if the commodi-

13 See F. B. Simon (1988/93): Unterschiede, die Unterschiede machen. Frankfurt (Suhrkamp); F. B. Simon (1990): My Psychosis, my Bicycle and I. The Self-Organisation of Madness. Northvale, NJ (Jason Aronson) 1996.

ties it supplies no longer find buyers. The survival of a living system depends not only on its own activities but also on those of its environment, or to put it better: on its own activities suiting those of the environment.

THE EXTERNAL PERSPECTIVE —
THE EMPLOYEE AS ENVIRONMENT OF THE ENTERPRISE

There are no systems "as such", there are merely observers who call something a "system", for example an enterprise, a division or the market. Observers differentiate and thereby distinguish units from an environment. If these units are made up of elements they can by called a "system"[14].

All too soon, anyone who studies an enterprise, the economy or the market as an observer has the agony of choice: What should he see as system, as an integral whole, what as element or part, what as the environment of this compound unit? This is not a matter of objectively right or wrong distinctions; the question is: Which of them are useful, which are more or less meaningful for what?

The answer to this question seems obvious: An enterprise consists of its employees and the means of production, its environment is then the market, which in turn consists of customers, etc. So the elements of the system "enterprise" are employees and workers combined in subsystems known as departments, works, divisions (or similar). These putative elements of the enterprise are often presented as flow charts at conferences and symbolised by small boxes. In the top box, for example, you find the word "executive", and under this the names of individual organisational units such as production, development, marketing. The importance of each and every employee within such a scheme can be measured by the number of colleagues he has to share his box with. (Experience shows that when such presentations are put on the table they have already been overtaken by the flow of events.) Moreover there are also the non-living parts and elements of the enterprise: factory buildings, machines, construction plans, trucks, bank accounts and other capital values or assets.

14 The term "system" derives from the Greek *syn* meaning "together" and *histein* meaning "put".

The disadvantage of such a model is that it does not simplify the complexity of enterprises and markets enough to give the top executives orientation for their everyday transactions. In order to make decisions, a manager needs a kind of mental map that gives him an idea of what information on the territory in which he moves he must definitely take into consideration and what he can imagine away with impunity; it must offer him guidelines from which he can assess where the choice of one or the other path might lead. It seems rather doubtful whether this can be deduced from such an organigram: With this usual method of distinction a manager is dealing with a great number of different elements, systems and an environment which are themselves highly complex. Their interrelations remain confusingly unfathomable; he can deduce no recipes for behaviour from this model.

The situation is quite different when you shift the focus of interest to what is important for decisions made by executives: one's own behaviour or that of others. Even if this goes directly against our habitual way of thinking, from the viewpoint of systems theory, behaviour can be seen as elements of an enterprise or of the market. Such systems are not made up of material, living or non-living components such as machines, administrative buildings, executive personnel or consumers, but of highly transient elements that have to be produced ever anew: the behaviour of people and machines.

The individual, whole person is thus to be seen not as part, but as the environment of an enterprise. The same is valid for the means of production: It is far more useful to consider them as environmental factors that form the prerequisites for the functioning of an enterprise without being a component of the enterprise themselves. Without the guarantee of these prerequisites, economic processes could no more take place than life could develop on earth without the necessary physical and chemical environmental conditions: no work without a person to do it. Only in Alice's Wonderland can the Cheshire cat disappear whilst its grin remains.[15] But not all of an employee's behaviour belong to the enterprise: Buying milk or watching television, eating, drinking or sleeping are all actions that are not elements of the enterprise.

---

15 L. Carroll (1865): Alice in Wonderland. London (Penguin) 1946.

To summarise: If no-one produced the behaviour that forms the enterprise and the market there would, of course, be no market and no enterprise. The systems enterprise and market do not, however, contain the machines that produce the commodities, nor do they contain the business partners who negotiate with each other, conclude contracts and effect payments. It is considerably more useful and simpler to consider only the behaviours produced by these people and machines – independent of who produces them.[16]

Environments of the enterprise

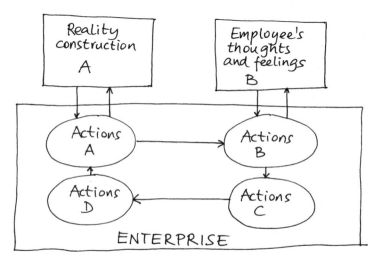

Fig. 6

To illustrate: The single body parts of an automobile can be screwed together by workers or by fully automatised robots. For the survival of the automobile factory, all that is important is that this behaviour is performed and co-ordinated at all. The same applies to administration, marketing, management as a whole: It is absolutely irrelevant who does what so long as what is necessary for the survival of the

16 See also N. Luhmann (1995): Social Systems. Stanford, CA (Stanford University Press).

firm is done. That does not mean that all behaviours produced in an enterprise are necessary for its survival. Some are even harmful and reduce the probability of survival. Nor does it mean that all these behaviours can be furnished by everyone in the same way and with the same quality: When a beginner starts working, the result might well turn out different to that of a crafty old hand; a sales manager of many years' standing will act differently in his new role as manager to the just as experienced marketing manageress.

It is thus advisable to see the executive as a person – and all the other employees – as an environment of the systems enterprise, division etc., not as their element. Someone who takes on responsibility for the success of this kind of system must think about what behaviour is necessary to lead it to success (or just to keep it alive) and what behaviour must be refrained from at all cost to avoid failure. To this end he must consider what the remaining environmental conditions in favour of one or the other are: How people in general (himself included), or the things whose behaviour he must calculate, function and who or what can and will produce which behaviour under which conditions.

With such an approach, the system, the entity enterprise can be compared to the match of a football team. In order to survive the season successfully, the production of certain patterns of behaviour is necessary. As many victories as possible need to be produced, that means scoring enough goals of their own and managing to prevent enough goals being scored against them. If they succeed in this, enough spectators come and buy tickets, TV companies broadcast the matches and finally the individual players receive undeservedly high salaries that allow them to get things straightened out with themselves and the world. This results in a good playing mood, they play fantastically well, score lots of goals, prevent goals against them, lots of spectators come to watch etc. And they all live happily ever after and are still top of the league. On the other hand, they might just as easily get self-satisfied, fat, lazy and greedy. They might prefer to occupy themselves with the fixed interests from the capital they have been able to invest as a result of undeservedly high salaries, with wine (cocaine), women and song. As a consequence they score fewer goals, indeed, on the contrary, lots of goals are scored against them, the spectators are frightened away etc. Although the individual players will not die from this, the enterprise will: The team is relegated from the first division, falls apart, rien ne va plus, the game is over ... The living system "the way team XY plays" dies because the necessary environment for its survival has been destroyed.

The popular subject of seminars "How can I motivate my employees?" thus proves to be a question of "conservation". A living system that destroys the environment necessary for its survival destroys itself.[17] All these correlations can be described from the perspective of the neutral external observer who – from the position of the spectator on the bleachers, so to speak – is observing the "Economy" game. He can, as it were, imagine the people away, construct abstract systems and reduce the fact of his own national team winning the World Cup to fortunately well-suited behaviour. This is the position from the view of theory and science. Everyone who has ever played football or been a manager himself knows that in practice it is not as easy to guide a team to its goal successfully as the fans' theories suggest: He can imagine away neither his fellow players nor himself but must live (survive) with them.

THE INNER PERSPECTIVE –
THE ENTERPRISE AS AN INDIVIDUAL'S ENVIRONMENT

If you are flying over the highway in a helicopter to ascertain where traffic is flowing unhindered and where there is congestion or stop-and-go traffic for the radio traffic service, the traffic seems – in particular where it is flowing – to be controlled by an invisible hand: At the slip roads and exits some automobiles join the flow of vehicles, others leave the line. A model highway, directed and remote-controlled by a resourceful do-it-yourself man might present a similar picture when seen from above. But as long-standing drivers and contributors to traffic jams, we know that there is no central area manager who has taken over the responsibility for controlling traffic and the expert planning and production of congestion. There is "only" the behaviour of the individual drivers which combines to form a pattern (congestion or no congestion). Traffic organises itself.

17 See G. Bateson (1971): The Cybernetics of Self. In: G. Bateson (1972): Steps to an Ecology of Mind. San Francisco (Chandler).

Every single driver behaves egotistically, that is, as though he were the center of the world. And yet one's own behaviour behind the wheel has to be coordinated with one's neighbour in order to prevent accidents. This is all the more successful the greater one's understanding that the other road-users also consider themselves the centre of the world. That is why an experienced chauffeur watches the car in front, looks in the rear mirror, looks left and right, accelerates, brakes, makes way. If every driver puts himself in the position of the other road-users and coordinates his behaviour with theirs, then traffic flows without hold-ups (provided certain external conditions are given, for example the road is wide enough, no Sunday drivers are on the road, no children run out in front of an automobile etc.).

Traffic, which from the outer perspective seems to be an ordered entity, arises from a number of individual, egocentric decisions of road-users, and not from some hierarchic, higher planning and controlling decision-making authority.

Let us have a look at what this means for the individual road-user who has no possibility to distance himself in an airplane, to gain the great overall view, who is not sitting on the bleachers, but has to play. Let us contrast his inner perspective of observation with the outer perspective. He can and must select his behaviour from the universe of all possible behaviours. In doing so, he must take into consideration that his behaviour not only contributes to producing or not producing a single social system: His actions gain importance for the maintenance or downfall of many different systems. To stay with this metaphor: Someone stuck in a traffic jam is not at work during this time, not with his family, not in the theatre. And in operating the gas pedal he not only contributes to building up or dissolving the traffic jam, but also to increasing air pollution, traffic noise etc. Whatever a person does can gain different meanings in different contexts.

The inner perspective of the person who contributes to the formation of systems of interaction by his behaviour must do justice to the manifold meaning of his actions, the diversity of the play area he is moving in. What seems good in one context can be rated bad in another. Someone who sits in his office working until midnight may perhaps earn a laurel wreath from his employer; but he is not likely to harvest much enthusiasm from his partner and the children, who may be longing for him to come home ...

His actions do not contribute to the production, maintenance and survival of one system, but can become effective as an element of several systems. From his inner perspective, there are probably weighty differences in the importance of the maintenance of these different systems. Today, preserving one's own life is probably more important for many people than preserving their firm, the prosperity of their own families more important than that of their native country. What combines all these systems is human behaviour, which has many different intentional and unintentional effects. What is useful for one system can harm the other.

Both enterprises and each individual employee can be seen as purposeful systems. By means of their organisational forms and behaviour, they try to secure their survival (economically or even physically). To do this they use each other as the means to an end: The enterprise's behaviour serves the employee, the employee's behaviour the enterprise. Ideally this gives rise to a synergy, a symbiotic mutual usefulness. It can, however, also lead to conflicting aims if behaviour serving a higher valued system from the individual perspective harms one that is subjectively less important.

THE INTEGRATION OF OUTER AND INNER PERSPECTIVE – BEHAVIOUR AS A COMMODITY

The radical market economy model provides an approach to integrating the inner and outer perspective of observation in a homogeneous concept.

Let us begin with the individual, whole person, or rather what we can perceive of him as an observer – from the outside. Ultimately we only see the part of him that lies outside the borders of his skin. We cannot look into his insides. He is a kind of nontrivial machine; we cannot directly observe him feeling or thinking, nor the biological processes that keep him alive. What we see is external characteristics and behaviour: his more or less well-groomed hair, the nervous twitch of his eyebrows, his polite greeting, slurred speech, his unrestrained swearing and nervous driving. Such descriptions of behaviour – the differentiation of various behaviours and their characterisation and assessment – allow different observers to come to an agreement, that is, their observations can be "objectified".

As we constantly produce units when making distinctions, we can see differentiated behaviour as well as real units as commodities (wares) which can be attributed a greater or lesser value. This view of behaviour is certainly nothing new, after all we are living in a service society. What is new is seeing *all* a person's behaviour as commodities: not only his or her work as chiropodist, doctor, hairdresser, management consultant etc. but also his sleeping, querulous grumbling, drinking, watching television, playing cards, inviting someone else to the cinema etc. All interactions between people, life as a whole, can – quite radically – be seen from the perspective of market economy.

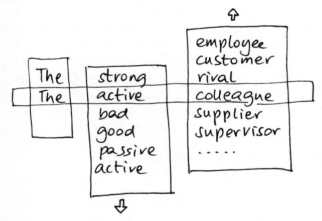

When differentiating we constantly produce units

Fig. 7

Every day we take our behaviour to market and exchange it for the behaviour of our fellow humans: The market for behaviour is an exchange market. Every individual is then comparable to an enterprise or a factory, continuously producing commodities and offering them on the free market: Action = transaction.[18]

There is no generally accepted currency on the market for behaviour: even money is only one of many means of exchange. This limits business relationships largely to the field of direct interaction. The exchange of behaviour takes place in accordance with the well tried example of barter-business: pipelines for natural gas.[19] If money plays any role at all, then only as an exception in the exchange of behaviour. Typical example: the "oldest trade" of the world – If you give me a behaviour – important and valuable to me – I will give you money.

This brings us to a specialty of this market that has far-reaching consequences. There is no abstract evaluation independent of the situation of the commodities to be traded (= behaviour). In every single case there has to be negotiation, in a concrete way and just for the current situation, here and now, on what behaviour is exchanged for what behaviour, and what behaviour is worth how much for which business partner. Each individual evaluates the behaviour (= commodity) produced by him or others according to his own individual and personal system of values.

Every individual is comparable to a state in which the currency is not freely convertible. It can be used within the borders of the respective state, but is of no use for transactions with the environment. It plays a role in the inner dynamics (on the psychological or biological level = inner structure and dynamics of a nontrivial machine), but has validity and value function only within the borders of this system which are closed to the outside.

---

18 That such an understanding is not totally unfounded is proved in the structures of our languages and their history. The term "factory" derives from the Latin *facere*, which means "to make, do". Business language shows traces of the identification of doing and transacting already effected in Latin: a factor is a person who carries on business transactions for another, factorage is a factor's commission etc.; see *Webster's New World Dictionary of the American Language,* p. 269, Concise Edition.

19 The term "barter," giving something in exchange for ... is derived from the Latin *prattare* (to exchange, cheat), which in turn has its origin in the Greek *práttein* (to make, do).

So in order to assess the subjective selection criteria for individual behaviour, we need merely consider the internal evaluation. This leads to the banal, but nevertheless revolutionary conclusion that the fact that someone produces certain behaviours proves that he has more or less consciously decided to behave this way (and not any other way); just as an enterprise that supplies certain commodities has obviously decided to supply these commodities. Every participant in the current exchange of behaviour always behaves in accordance with his own inner evaluation of the behaviour (= commodity) to be paid for and received, that is in accordance with his view of supply and demand. In this sense every human being behaves in an economically rational way at all times and in all places.

This does not mean that his decisions were or needed to be rationally and economically meaningful from the view of the external "objective" observer. They might even seem absolutely mad and absurd. But from the inner perspective of someone who always has to make new decisions on his behaviour and make a selection among the possibilities at his disposal, they are always rational. He always acts in an economically optimal way according to his current assessment, dependent on the situation and his knowledge of the state of the market.

The evaluation of such decisions must inevitably differ according to whether it occurs from the inner or outer perspective. It results from the diverse standards of value which every observer takes as a basis depending on the perspective.

However, the lack of a freely convertible currency comparable to money for the direct exchange of behaviour has far-reaching consequences. Money enables value to be put into concrete terms and objectified, that is, taken out of the current context of interaction[20], to combine past and future, to use tomorrow the value created today. It is something like a memory, a material symbol with which the difference between past and present, present and future can be cancelled out. A value obtained today in one business relationship can be saved and stored in the form of money so that it gains a certain degree of

---

20 See F. B. Simon (1984): Der Prozeß der Individuation. Göttingen (Vandenhoeck & Ruprecht) p. 191 pp.

constancy independent of time and can be used tomorrow in a different business relationship.[21]

The possibilities of doing this are very limited in the direct, cashless exchange of behaviour. A different, more concrete form of keeping an account and of memory takes its place: *Each individual keeps - more or less consciously – give and take accounts for all partners in interaction in his own private currency.*

In his own private bank each individual keeps a debit and credit account for each partner – whether this person wants it or not (maybe the chosen partner doesn't even know our banker). When he gives a partner something, does or achieves something "for this person", he books a debit under this person's account number; the partner now owes him something in compensation to the value of the service done for this partner.

The shadow of past and future, that is, the state of the accounts of all participants in the bookkeeping of all participants, flows into current business relationships. Not every commodity sold is paid for immediately, not every good or bad deed is rewarded or punished immediately. Nevertheless, in interaction, debit and credit are always balanced, credit lines stipulated and debts sued for: *Patterns of interaction arise from the interplay between the pattern of balancing accounts and the state of accounts of all participants in the interaction.*

In a relationship with other people (both with individuals and with groups) it is possible to make investments or to save, to pay out or receive interest. These, too, are paid or claimed back in the form of behaviour. If a person behaves differently towards different people and expects different things from them, the reason is that their debit and credit accounts have different balances in his bookkeeping.[22]

However, value can not only be attributed to what one does, but also to what one does not do. The exchange value of behaviour can

---

21 See J. M. Keynes (1936): The General Theory of Employment, Interest and Money. London (Macmillan).
22 The Hungarian-American family therapist Ivan Boszormenyi-Nagy has stressed in great detail the importance of debit and credit accounts for the dynamics of family interaction even through several generations; see I. Boszormenyi-Nagy a. G. Spark (1973): Invisible Loyalties: Reciprocity in Intergenerational Family Therapy. New York (Harper & Row).

consist in the very fact of not doing something unpleasant or undesired (In their relationship to their creator, Adam and Eve in paradise could only offer not picking and eating the apple from the tree of knowledge in exchange. Everything else was allowed in their relationship to God, that is, it made no difference to him). The quality of a person's behaviour patterns can consist in the very fact that he does not manifest certain behaviours. He never quarrels, never protests, never contradicts, never expresses deviating opinions, never thinks about the sense or nonsense of orders etc.

On the other hand, though, some behaviours cannot really be treated as commodities. *They are better comparable to the waste from the production of material products.* Eating, drinking and sleeping are examples for behaviour not usually included in an exchange. However, these can also be bartered when, for example, a prominent political prisoner or the daughter of a good family decides to go on a hunger strike. He or she then refrains from doing something that is tacitly assumed to be normal and self-evident and thus not rated as a commodity, so that the re-establishment of the behaviour normally manifested gains in value.

The rating and exchange of behaviour are closely connected to the process of constructing reality. This in turn is governed to a great extent by focussing attention on communication.[23] The principle "What the eye does not see, the heart cannot grieve over!" is valid the same here as in the case of marketing any other products. *Wares are only what we are aware of.* Behaviour that is not distinguished or labelled differently can have no communicative meaning and rating. Wares we are not aware of cannot be traded.

If a supervisor – although he regards the work of his employees highly – does not expressly appreciate, reward or praise it because he assumes that the employees are well aware of his appreciation, he runs the risk of them not working well in future. He offers nothing in exchange.

---

23 The words "awareness" and "ware" have their roots in the Anglo Saxon *gewaer, waer* meaning "cautious" (see *Websters New World Dictionary*, Concise Edition, p. 52) and are closely related to the Middle High German *warn,* meaning "pay attention" (see F. Kluge: Etymologisches Wörterbuch. Berlin (de Gruyter) 1975, p. 832 and 838).

Material things, too, only have a value because someone gives them a personal value. In this sense, money is first of all only a commodity like any other. However, it is distinguished by its almost universal exchangeability and temporal constancy, so that it can find a use as a means of communication for value. In the spectrum of exchanged commodities, it constitutes the extreme example of interchangeability and is opposed at the opposite end of the spectrum by concrete, unique and unmistakable behaviour.

Thus when speaking of value, we must distinguish which area of phenomena we want to comment on. The so-called exchange value is the respective currently attainable market value for behaviour towards a certain opposite number and depends on his system of values.

Example

At a management meeting the lack of electronic data processing support, which has already resulted in an increase in customer complaints, is criticised. A sales manager says: "It's no wonder. We have so many problems with our electronic data processing that we have to work out lots of things with a pocket calculator."

The marketing manageress takes this up and criticises the present difficult situation yet again. The managing director (the overall boss) answers defensively: "The way you treat your employees the situation is problematic anyway ..."

The electronic data processing topic is thus put aside for a while until a young division manager presents the electronic data processing problem in similar words to the marketing boss. To this the managing director says: "Yes, yes, I know, I've been trying to find a solution to that already ..." and explains what he has done so far.

The consequence of this sequence is the following rule: "If you have anything to criticise try and get the support of the young division manager and avoid the help of the (female) marketing boss!"

From the outer perspective of the spectator on the bleachers observing the interaction, "price lists" can be set up in this as in any other situation, that is, sequences of interaction and behavioural exchange sequences can be described. What value the participants in the interaction attribute positively or negatively to the individual

43

behaviours cannot be observed directly from the outside (it is only accessible to self-observation) and can merely be inferred from the behaviour.

In the situation described here a market established itself in which there was a sharp fall in prices for the criticism of the marketing manageress. Critical statements were a commodity that she produced in abundance (in particular towards her own employees) so that a devaluation resulted: There was no more "buying". The young division manager, whose criticism was more seldom, supplied a scarce commodity which was thus rated higher.

In general, the exchange model can be applied to the interaction of a living system with its environment (e. g. an employee with his firm, or even vice versa: a firm with its employee). Invoices are always presented, benefit must be paid for with cost. However, in such a relationship the terms of payment are usually longer than in interaction between individuals, and the relationship between cost and benefit is less transparent since the consequences of behaviour are often very diffuse and not directly ascertainable. Moreover, they are usually claimed back a lot later. But even here fact is: All behaviour has some sort of consequence, that is, everything has its price.

When you apply such a radical market economy model the difference between economy and ecology, between epistemology and ethics dissolves: At all times and in all places life is then a question of evaluations.

As every observer makes his own evaluations according to his non-convertible currency no-one can refer to any kind of objective values and claim to know what is right and good, wrong and bad etc.

The radical market economy model offers a possibility to describe the rules of a system of interaction, the complexity and interconnection of interaction from the external perspective – like in Monopoly. It shows which moves are rated high and low and for which products (behaviour) in the short or long term what prices must be paid. But it also reveals understanding for individual decisions running counter to the predicted rationality of this market. For it takes the autonomy of the involved individuals into account, that is, their internal standards and the various markets on which they offer their behaviour. Moreover, it focuses attention on the historical dimension of interaction by taking into consideration mutual accounting on former merits and returns expected in the future that have an effect in the here and now.

RECIPES

- *Differentiate between menu and meal, between words and deeds! If you want to know what someone thinks, then listen less to what he says and keep a closer watch on what he does (that also applies to you yourself, of course).*
- *Be wary of all abstractions and empty words, they are always ambiguous! Whenever you are confronted by any kind of concept ("peak performance", "success" etc.) translate them into behaviour: Draw a circle on a sheet of paper and write inside the circle from what behaviour of which person you would recognise that this term can be used (for example, if you are "successful" the chauffeur holds the door open for you – and a lot of other people behave characteristically, you yourself as well, probably); and outside the circle write down your own and other peoples' behaviours connected with the fact that this concept does not fit ("unsuccessful" then means, for example, that you have no time to read the novel you have always wanted to read, no money to go on holiday etc.). Set up cost-benefit accounts for the production of both sides of the differentiation!*
- *Again carefully considering cost and benefit, decide what you focus your attention on every day and what you wish to observe. This choice will change the world! What do you need to know, what can you ignore and what ought you better ignore completely?*
- *Reckon with the unpredictability of the world! Dispense with security and be content with probability. Never try to see through or understand anything utterly!*

3. Organisation

"The word organisation is a noun and also a myth. If you look for an organisation you won't find one. What you will find is ... connected incidents that seep through concrete walls ..."
Karl E. Weick[1]

*"We have lost Shiva, the dancer of Hinduism whose dance at the trivial level is both creation and destruction but in whole is beauty.
We have lost Abraxas, the terrible and beautiful god of both day and night in Gnosticism.
We have lost totemism, the sense of parallelism between man's organisation and that of the animals and plants."*
Gregory Bateson[2]

THE HOUSEWIFE AND THE ARTIST –
CREATING, MAINTAINING AND DISINTEGRATING ORDER

In principle there are two different types of human activities or work. The first gains the attention of the observer when it is being done, the second is only noticed when it is not done. In both cases events are created that contribute to what we then, all in all, call "organisation": a system of coordinated behaviour.[3]

Let us begin with a few examples of the second type of achievement. Because the term is so nice and handy, we will call it "house-

1   K. Weick (1969): Social Psychology of Organising. Reading, MA (Addison-Wesley).
2   G. Bateson (1979): Mind and Nature. A Necessary Unity. New York (Dutton), Bantom Edition 1980.
3   See K. Weick (1969).

46

wifery": washing up that hasn't been done, apartments that haven't been tidied up, rubbish bins that smell terrible when they haven't been emptied, roads in which the pot-holes haven't been repaired, forgotten oil changes, letters with the first paragraph not written, missing signatures on transfer forms so the wages couldn't be transferred, babies that haven't been fed ... – all of these are the more or less noticeable results of housewifery not done. It should be obvious that it is not a question of sex-specific tasks in the biological sense. We have purposely chosen the term "housewifery" to characterise this type of organisational achievement because in our society, more often than not, such jobs are done by women – particularly in the private area, but to a great extent within companies as well. It is they who, in accordance with their traditional role, are often assigned and take on responsibility for the creation and maintenance of a natural order.

As long as these kinds of activities are done they are literally invisible. If we compare the organisation of human co-existence and co-working with the functioning of a living organism, the processes maintained by housewifery are comparable to circulation and metabolism. They ensure the natural maintenance of the structures within the boundaries of the skin. We do not usually notice that we digest until we suffer from constipation, that we breathe until we are breathless etc. Awareness of these activities contributing to the creation of a natural order does not arise until they no longer function.There are differences in the importance of these processes and structures for survival: We can live well without an appendix, after a fashion without a leg, but not at all without the activities of the head, heart or liver.

Like the body, every organisation and every enterprise requires certain processes to create and maintain their infrastructures. Social order is not something self-evident that comes from above, but rather the extremely improbable result of human behaviour. And if no-one is there to produce this behaviour over and over again, order disintegrates. A machine that is not serviced loses its ability to function. Laws that are not enforced lose their practical validity. A targeted state that is not controlled is not constant or does not become the actual state. Deviating behaviour that is not sanctioned leads to a change of the standards and rules and thus to an alteration of order, or even to disorder and chaos. Housewifery in this sense is conservative, it ensures predictability. Its results are transient and have "of themselves" absolutely no eternal value. Only its constant repetition, its regularity gives it a value outlasting time, whereby the single deed – every single time the washing-up is done and thus whoever has washed the dishes – is forgotten.

As counterpart to this type of ordering work, the activities of all kinds of "trouble-makers" or rather their extreme form, "terrorists", need to be mentioned here. Every disturbance threatens the given order. The political intention of terrorist attacks is destructive and aims at the disintegration of the existing order. Where trust in the self-evidence of its rules is no longer given, the complexity of the world increases. It seems chaotic, unpredictable and unordered.

A third form of behaviour, the effect of which is something like a compromise between the seemingly insurmountable differences between housewifery and terrorist disturbances, is the work of an "artist" or "inventor". Even here it is, of course, not a question of a biological prerequisite when we speak of "the artist". The fact that relatively few women are recognised as artists should not lead to false inferences.

The special merit of the work of artists is that it is not self-evident and cannot be interchanged. Its results (even if they are not always pleasant) are noticeable because in some way they transcend the limits of the familiar order, often even run counter to it and disturb it. They creatively produce something new, something unprecedented. Insofar as the products of such activities are material things (houses, pictures, books, music, drafts, production plans etc.), they can outlast time so that future generations can bind laurel wreaths for their creators or pay them royalties. In this kind of work it is the individual deed that counts, the creation. It lives on, and if he is lucky, after accomplishing the deed its creator can lead an idle life on a South Sea island. The social effect of these creative activities is sometimes disquieting; they disturb the familiar order, deviate from the norm of what is natural and give birth to unpredictability. At the same time, though, this very kind of activity is responsible for something new, it brings innovation and broadens a system's repertoire of action with new options.

If we try to characterise the attributes of these two ideally typical behaviours in a few key-words, we get the following table:

Housewifery	Artists' Work
(Preservation - enabling change)	(Change - on the basis of the preserver)
Maintenance of an existing order - establishing security	Disturbance of an existing order - establishing uncertainty
Production and maintenance of structures	Dissolving structures
reliable, normative, conservative	surprising, not normative, innovative
Normality, rigidity	Madness, flexibility
Confirmation of expectations, predictability	Expectations disappointed, unpredictability
Peace and order	Unrest, chaos

Fig. 8

In order to illustrate the difference between these two forms of the effect of individual behaviour in organisations we now present a few examples from the everyday life of an enterprise.

Neutralising deviations and maintaining order versus deviation amplifying and alteration of the existing order: The patriarch of the firm's inexhaustible brainwaves on the golf course and the sporadic *fireworks* that he lets off in the company (buying machines after tours of the company, instructions and orders valid immediately etc.) have to be distinguished as "possible" or "not possible" by the person appointed to hold the fort, in other words his assistant, in order to translate them into instructions for action that the company can deal with. Otherwise they would probably have a "terrorist" effect.

Our patriarch's secretary transcribes the minutes of the monthly strategy meetings attended only by the top line of the hierarchy level. She collects the results of the distributed homework and gives the contents of the reports to the project managers, whose places are formally on the third hierarchic level, so that they can bring their projects into line with the agreed targets. Here it is the secretary without

49

whose activities the structures necessary for realising strategies would not be produced or rather maintained.

The effect on possible options – reliable, normative, conservative versus surprising, not conservative, innovative: Traditionally, in enterprise cultures with a strong division of labour, plants are only serviced when the controls indicate "minimum", "tolerance exceeded" etc. – and only then; or when the service plans of a division from the third storey of the administration building provide for it; then, but only then, the plant is always serviced. This way nothing happens very often unless a part of a machine breaks before the end of its predicted life span. But this way the plant stands still first for servicing, a second time for changing tools, a third time for changing the chuck for a new line and possibly a fourth time because it's time for a break; and yet there's system behind all this: it all accords with the reliable "housewifery" norms of four different divisions.

The "artistic" solution to the plant's servicing and standstill problems: The coordination of servicing and maintenance with changing tools and chuck and other machine standstills in order to minimise the plant's total standstills would be most likely to succeed if the responsibility for these various activities were transferred from the divisions to the plant's operators. From the point of view of the divisions, however, this kind of reorganisation is always connected with a violation of the given norms. Yet seen from a higher standpoint, its effect is destructive (for the division's order) and constructive (for the company as a whole) at the same time.

On the other hand, someone who predominantly manifests behaviour whose effect is considered destructive for the enterprise is not seen as an artist, but as a "mere trouble-maker" and sooner or later excluded. For this reason we do not need to occupy ourselves any closer with the "terrorist" pattern of behaviour. However, artists are only too often suspected of terrorism when the positive effect of their disturbances is not seen.

As can easily be seen from these few examples, the behaviour "housewifery" is a question of negative feedback mechanisms. In contrast, "disturbance" is a positive feedback. Whereas deviations are balanced and the existing order confirmed in the first case, in the second deviations are amplified. In the case of the activity of an artist or inventor both occur. Deviations from order are amplified and yet order – a new order – is created.

The cocktail of meanings connected with these ideal types of activities – housewifery and artistic activity – within an enterprise could be extended considerably. In the list of examples presented here, allocations from the outer perspective of the unconcerned observer and from the inner perspective of those concerned are mixed. The nearer they come to the inner perspective, the more ideological connotations their judgements acquire. Preserving traditional structures versus innovation, these are the two apparently incompatible poles and aims towards which not only political parties, but also all others responsible for decision-making in organisations are oriented.

If we look at living systems, it becomes clear that one of their unmistakable characteristics is that they hold both tendencies in a dynamic balance. They are organised paradoxically. They get their order by being in a position to disintegrate it. The body survives and keeps its form by changing. It is well known that a palm tree that sways in the wind is far more stable than a mast that breaks. Living systems are organised antagonistically, they survive because they combine contradictory tendencies causing order and chaos.[4]

In principle, an organisation that lives in an unchangeable and stable environment, an enterprise, an institution or a family, for example, does not need to change itself either. In this theoretical case, activities maintaining the traditional order suffice for survival. Unfortunately this is extremely seldom the case today. Such conditions were given for native tribes living in a hardly changing jungle environment cut off from the outer world.

Here and now, in our fast moving society, this applies mostly to institutions whose behaviour serves to satisfy some of the most elementary human needs. Schools, official authorities, even restaurants, hospitals, brothels and prisons etc. have changed their patterns of interaction and internal structures only very slightly over the years. So long as their environments, i. e. their customers, allow it, they need not learn anything, or only little, and can remain as they are to a surprising extent.

To express it in terms of radical market economy: There is always a market for their behaviour; just as eating and drinking are essential for the individual organism, such organisations require cer-

---

4   In this connection Edgar Morin speaks of "systemic antagonism", see E. Morin (1992): Method: Towards a Study of Humankind. New York (Lang).

tain activities to maintain their order and structure. Someone who wants to "play it safe" and have a guaranteed market for exchanging his own products (behaviour, activities, work) ought to look for a job in this field. On the level of society as a whole, this kind of housewifery is the traditional task of government employees. The other side of such a choice, however, is that the non-visibility of the production of things taken for granted leads to this kind of work having a low or no rating. It is not seen as an achievement, but taken for granted as given. For the person performing the work this results in unfavourable market conditions for exchanging his behaviour: something no-one is aware of does not become a ware. The fact that the activities of air-traffic controllers or rubbish collectors are not indispensable does not enter public consciousness until the air-traffic controllers "work to rule" or the rubbish collectors go on strike.

The situation is different in the free economy. Here there is no guaranteed market at all, neither for a firm's products nor for the behaviour of its employees. Even in enterprises there are, of course, more or less exchangeable activities, and the degree of this exchangeability or non-exchangeability determines the lower or higher market value of each employee's activities. On the whole, however, for the organisation of economic enterprises it is a fact that their survival is not secure and their environment not constant. The market on which they have to prove themselves changes. Supply and demand are not constant, and in general no firm holds a monopoly for a product, in contrast to an authority.

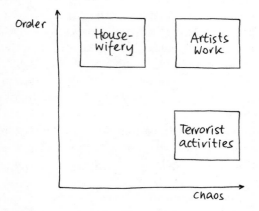

Fig. 9

An enterprise that enters the free market thus requires both house-wifery and artistic activity. Only then can it change sufficiently to maintain its stability in a dynamically changing world. The faster the market changes, the more flexibly and quicker the enterprise needs to react, change its internal structures, learn and develop creative potentials. An enterprise in the computer branch, for example, in which technology is developing at a rapid pace, will have to organise a different relationship between creative and conservative tendencies than a factory for garden gnomes, for which production procedures and markets remain stable over the years.

In a diagram these different forms of organisation can be presented as a "field of conflict" or "force field" in which ordering forces that remove deviations or innovative forces that amplify deviations gain preponderance respectively and perform a more important function.

If the organisation of an enterprise does not want to remain flexible, it has to find an optimal combination of behaviour for current and future environmental conditions which effects order and chaos and combines these two contradicting tendencies. Herein lies the art of management.

The conflict between these two organisational tendencies shows itself mainly in the seemingly insurmountable prejudice of employees in the development division of an enterprise against those in production, the disagreement between the marketing and the finance division, between those who back growth and those who demand consolidation of what has been achieved. The former are full of new ideas, the latter are happy to have the old ideas "under control" at last. However, this conflict is not only unavoidable, but expedient. There is simply no best combination of these two tendencies for all time, independent of situation. Over and over again a solution "fitting" the conditions of survival (= market) has to be renegotiated in conflict.

TEAMWORK –
DIVISION OF LABOUR AND COOPERATION

All famous teams in world history consisted of people with very contradictory characteristics and abilities: Adam and Eve, Laurel and

Hardy, Romeo and Juliet, Terence Hill and Bud Spencer, Winnetou and Old Shatterhand, Bonny and Clyde. In their smallest form, these more or less spontaneously developing partnerships represent the basic model of an organisation in which mutual ventures are coordinated.

An organisation consists of events which (among other things) are produced by the behaviour of people and machines. In view of the fact that a day lasts only 24 hours and cannot be made much longer even if we count the night, the possibility of producing events is very limited for individual people. A second limiting factor is that not everyone has the ability to produce all kinds of events. A somewhat compulsive, exact and precise person might possibly make a good accountant, but it is doubtful whether he would be just as successful in compiling the strategic guidelines of the company's policy or in managing the development office.

Wherever events or behaviour are required that transcend the capacities of individuals, an organisation ensues, i. e. the behaviour of several people is combined in such a way that they interlock, follow on from each other and become a process, a pattern of interaction, a game that can be described by certain rules.

The ability of such an organisation can exceed that of individual people because it uses and coordinates the differences between the potentials of the individuals. Seemingly incompatible differences, for example housewifery and disturbances of law and order, can be united to form a functional artistic whole.

One of the consequences of this kind of division of labour and cooperation is that it inevitably promotes specialising. The differences between what individuals do are getting bigger and bigger. First of all, everyone does what he can do particularly well, he refines his product and fosters the market niche for his abilities. But in the course of time, these structures solidify, they become order, sustained by collective expectations and established by rigid role standards. Finally, it may be that such standards and expectations limit the development options of individuals. Their abilities are no longer used optimally, and finally specialisation and one-track minds hinder cooperation.

Family life can be seen as an organisation, too. The male and female roles in the family provide a good and clear example of the

advantages and disadvantages of division of labour and cooperation. Single parents know how exacting it is to have to do everything
on their own, not to be able to delegate anything, never to be able to
discover with surprise that something has already been done without it having to be him/her who did it. Teamwork between two partners allows both greater freedom and life can be organised more economically. They don't both have to do the shopping or pay for their
own apartment with an expensive bathroom suite. However, the fact
is only too easily lost to view that the specialisation connected with
both roles is mutually dependent (traditionally: "The man goes out
into the hostile world ... and the able housewife, the children's
mother, works in the home ..."). Freed from duties in the home, the
partner who goes out into the hostile world (it can, of course, also be
the woman), can plunge into the world of employment and depend
on the table being laid, the apartment heated, the meal cooked and
probably even the bed warmed when he/she gets home in the evening; and the one who stays at home and does the dishes doesn't
need to worry about earning money, because this is done by his/her
partner.

Meanwhile this distribution of roles is no longer so rigid and
firm in the family and in the coexistence of men and women. It no
longer fits the environment, i. e. the needs of the participants. The
reason this example is presented in so much detail is as follows: It
serves to illustrate the concept of "collaboration" (teamwork).[5] This
model from family research describes how partners often resolve a
conflict they both have, for example the ambivalence between the
desire for bonding and security on the one hand and fear of losing
their individual freedom in an obligating union on the other. They
achieve this by attributing the two sides of the ambivalence, the conflict, to one partner respectively as a characteristic; one partner then
acts as though he or she were free of all conflicting feelings, had always wanted eternal proximity between the partners ("Love me ten-
der, love me true, never let me go"), while the other insists on his
freedom. One clings, the other seems constantly in flight from the
prison of a reliable bond.

---

5 See J. Willi (1975): Die Zweierbeziehung. Reinbek (Rowohlt).

From the inner perspective of a co-actor in this partnership drama, each has the impression of being stricken by fate with a partner who doesn't suit him, who always wants the exact opposite of what he himself wants. From the outer perspective, it becomes clear that each needs the other to stay free of ambivalence, free of conflicting desires and feelings. If the one did not cling, the other could not sense his desire to flee, but would possibly have to realise that he, or rather she, also sought reliability and security; and vice versa, if he or she did not constantly manifest his/her desire for freedom and independence, his/her partner would realise that he/she also had such wishes and that the idea of a secure relationship is not only pleasant, but also frightening. The ambivalence of both concerned is organised "away" in their interaction within the whole system of partnership, both contradictory tendencies are represented and remain in balance. At the same time each of the two co-workers in this organisation can do what he or she does best (and possibly learn to do it ever better): clinging or fleeing, fighting for the preservation of the existing order or for innovation.

If such organisational forms with division of labour and cooperation did not arise spontaneously (self-organisation) one would have to invent them. The risk involved, however, is that the participants, from the inner perspective of the co-players, develop an all too simple world view. There are no ambivalences in their picture of themselves or others, every person is attributed clearly identifiable characteristics that are really the result of interaction between several people. Who manifests what behaviour in such patterns of interaction is actually completely irrelevant. The main thing is that what has to be done actually gets done. A living system as a whole must always acknowledge all the necessary functions for its survival.

Here is one of the exemplary stories taken straight from life (living together):

An employee in an IT-division who worked in an office near his home was constantly annoyed at his wife's lack of independence and criticised that the task of dealing with everything to do with maintaining structures always fell to him. Her lack of independence was terrible, but it was the only really bad part of the relationship. She accepted her lack of independence and admired her husband for his purposeful behaviour.

When he was promoted and frequently working outside the office or abroad, he suddenly began to criticise a change in his wife within his circle of friends. She was different now, she was no longer as charming and affectionate. Somehow she took too little notice of him and did not appreciate his new, exacting job.

What had happened? As long as the husband was "at home" he, the self-made man, the man of action, saw to everything outside the household, in particular in areas where he found an audience. Then he found admirers in his customers abroad and could no longer fulfil the tasks maintaining structure – apart from bringing home the money – for the simple reason that he was only present sporadically during the week. His wife, formerly so lacking independence, automatically filled this gap and visibly took over his former functions of maintaining the system, at times even surprising herself. She dealt with the authorities, called in workers for the house, dealt with all the business at the bank etc. She had her own audience and admirers who perceived her new behaviour and among other things she had found herself. The market situation for her behaviour had changed radically. The market value for affection had dropped, that for self-responsible activities had risen, the roles of both partners changed …

When certain actions have to be done over and over again, the development of roles is likely. The fact that someone does something once increases the probability that he will do it a second time. He now has the appropriate preliminary experience, he learns, gains new abilities; he has developed a product (behaviour), and it is only logical to make use of its market value. For everyone else the effort to take over his activity is much greater than for him. A mechanism has been started up that lessens deviation. Certain expectations develop as to who should do what: "We've always done it that way …!"

A social order has developed, not planned by anyone, but nevertheless effective. Certain expectations are directed to each of the participants which define his scope of action – a projection of the experiences of the past into the future. These expectations determine what he may or may not do, and they are combined with tacit attributions of personal characteristics. After all, one needs – according to the logic behind it – certain qualities (or the lack of certain qualities) to manifest or refrain from certain behaviours.

If these expectations and attributions are then removed from the original, concrete person, a role results. Another person can slip into his place, the expectations and attributions tell him what behaviour is required, what he must "be like" in order to preserve a functioning organisation. The result is a job description. This reduces the complexity of the system for all concerned. As the view from the outer perspective is generally not accessible to them – the bigger and more complex the system, the less it is possible to keep "everything" in view and act at the same time – they receive a limited frame for their activities as co-players on which they can focus their attention and in which they can orientate themselves.

From the total system, a multicorporate enterprise with an immense number of participants, for example, one segment (the market) is taken out in which they – absolutely free of ambivalence – know who they are dealing with and what behaviour they must contribute to the exchange: For example, one person has only to see to the development of new products or economical budgeting, only deal with employees XYZ, but never with UVW. He knows which exchange partner he must respect and with whom he must cooperate. Like the automobile driver in heavy traffic, he can limit himself to watching the drivers closest to him and suit his driving to theirs.

Anyone who is closely attached to the inner perspective of his co-player inevitably loses the correlations and connections in their entirety from his range of vision (if they were ever there in the first place).

Nevertheless, this kind of established organisational structure is generally useful as it provides prescriptive rules and automatisms. The problem of who does what need not be discussed over and over again. Areas of competence are clearly demarcated, interaction is regulated. The total system can achieve a degree of complexity which far supersedes the cognitive capacity of all individuals involved.

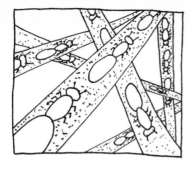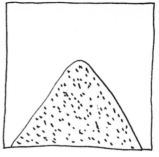

Anyone who is stuck in the inner perspective inevitably loses the overall view.

Fig. 10

Within an organisation, roles serve to guarantee certain behaviours. They are defined as far as content is concerned by expected activities and as far as relationships are concerned by the combination with expected activities from other roles (the commodities to be provided by other role-bearers).

If these commodities are rated differently within the organisation, the roles and the people holding them will also be rated differently. Leading roles and minor roles and their relationships to one another are formally established. The organigram, the description and rating of positions, is born.

Organisational rules, or rather structures and processes, are about joint automatisms of action that represent something like undisputed positions. They help to simplify coping with daily life in the company and to guarantee structures once optimised in their efficiency over a long period of time.

The advantage, but also the danger of organised processes lies in the shortening and simplification of everyday events given by such automatisms of action and schemata. They can also be long obsolete and preserve events that are no longer optimal. Yesterday's organisational solution requires improvement by tomorrow. Important environments such as customers, suppliers, the legal system, employees' families, the employees themselves manifest their nontriviality and do not stick to what is expected of them. Currencies decline, values change, so that once profitable commodities on the market of activities can lead to negative entries on the accounts of those concerned.

It often seems difficult enough to develop alternative models to the traditional division in male and female roles in the family, although it is only a question of a limited number of behaviours and relationships that need to be renegotiated between only two people. However, it is much more difficult in an enterprise. The number of things to be done and the number of people involved is very much greater, the evolving system far more complex.

THE LUCKY-DIP EFFECT –
THE BEHAVIOUR OF PEOPLE AS ENTITIES AND ITS RATING

You cannot kiss an enterprise. Much less can you employ a certain behaviour. You can only indirectly ensure that an organisation is preserved by acquiring the means of producing behaviour. You have to buy the cow, even if you only need one litre of milk. You have to employ people as entities, with head and hair, faults and quirks, even if you only want certain services and achievements from them. This is the chance and also the risk of every organisation, every enterprise.

You go into a shop, so to speak, to buy a certain commodity, a special kind of behaviour, but you only get the desired product if you buy a whole parcel of other articles at the same time. This is where unpredictability comes in. Normally you cannot pick out the contents of this lucky-dip; it may be full of useful products that further the development of the organisation, or full of annoying and troublesome products.

The individual is autonomous, i. e. he acts according to his own inner values, his own personal reality construction, his own world view, his own motives and aims. He is a nontrivial machine whose behaviour is principally unpredictable and not controllable from the outside. And yet the seemingly improbable succeeds: several people working together, producing predictable, interlocking courses of action.

The explanation for this is simple: Every single person who contributes to organised behaviour has "sold" his nontriviality. He forgoes using his unpredictability and on the basis of his own decision behaves as though he were taxable and predictable. He adheres to the rules of the game although he doesn't actually have to. And he does this because it pays off, because it is economically sensible and because the cost-benefit account in his personal currency is to his advantage.

Example: A department store in the fashion business with 17 categories of goods such as ladies' coats, outdoor wear, accessories, ... for example, introduces new planning methods which considerably reduce the decision-making responsibilities of the representatives of the different categories. They put up a fight and try to get round the new planning methods. They insist on their nontriviality. The representatives of one category of goods (accessories) don't have this problem. They adapt ideally to the new methods.

Explanation: This category of goods is not considered so important within the department store. The profit of selling one's nontriviality consists in the attention, interest and respect that the directors grant the faultless functioning of the new planning methods.

In this case, the division and every single one of its employees has a similar gain. This is not the rule, however. Just as each individual employee is the means to an end for the organisation, an environmental factor necessary for survival – like the air we breathe –, the organisation is always the means to an end for the individual employee and only in extremely rare cases the end itself. It is not the mutual definition of aims that make people cooperate, but rather the mutual means. Each employee in an enterprise has his own internally defined values. What connects them all is the mutual road to realising these different values: the enterprise.[6]

However, not everything that serves the realisation of these different, individual aims and values seems at first sight to serve the aims of the enterprise as well. The employees of an organisation always produce more, or rather different behaviours than are theoretically actually necessary to maintain the organisation (they visit the restroom, flirt with each other, yawn, do crossword puzzles, snooze, gossip about colleagues, phone their aunt etc.). But they may possibly think about improving production methods, new products and

6   See K. Weick (1969): Social Psychology of Organising. Reading, MA (Addison-Wesley).

more favourable organisational functioning (quote from a marketing manager: "I get my best ideas in the bath"), although this, too, is not part of their closely specified range of duties as set out in their job description – if they have one. And there is another factor: Possibly the idea for the new product comes to employee XY while gossiping with colleague Z during working hours. Over and above this the employees of an organisation foster relationships which are not only not provided for in the organisation's planning, but are even undesired, since they informally question the formal structure (the female manager of division X sleeps with the officer in charge of division Y outside of working hours). But this – pillow talk – possibly means that the flow of information between the divisions is improved in an unplanned and unpredictable way. Short-term and theoretically negatively rated behaviours of employees can have positive effects in the long-term – and vice versa, of course. This is a lucky-dip effect which is beyond any kind of planning and entails the potential for the rise and fall of an enterprise.

Since the elements of an enterprise (activities) can never be acquired directly and incorporated in a total construction, the structure of an organisation can never function in accordance with the engineer model. All planning must therefore be vague and ambiguous, unpredictability must be taken into account. It has to content itself with marking out a frame that limits the freedom of the individual jobholder where this freedom could have damaging effects, without blocking it where it might be useful. This means planning has to be content with establishing what must be done on all accounts and what must definitely be refrained from. This leads to the question of what importance and what value is or must be attributed to what behaviour of which employee at which time and in which position.

At this point, a very serious difference between the inner and outer perspective of observation shows up. This may be clarified by another example:

While planning a new hospital building, among other things cooperation between the laboratory or rather the laboratory assistants and the nursing staff on the wards was examined. This revealed that the course of work was organised as follows: Every morning, one of the nurses brought blood or urine samples from each ward to the laboratory in the basement. In order to get to the laboratory they had to use the lift or the stairs, which took a great deal longer but was, strangely enough, favoured. After a few minutes walk they reached the laboratory situated in an annex. Here they gave a laboratory employee the samples together with the respective laboratory slips determining which tests were required. Generally, handing over the samples was combined with a less formal exchange of information. The nursing staff thus provided background information on the patients the tests were being done for: from their diagnoses to their current state of health, from the course of the illness to the problems the doctor treating this patient was having with him. Apart from this, other gossip ("which doctor is doing it with which nurse...") was exchanged. About five to ten minutes passed ("the length of a cigarette") until handing over the samples was completed. On the whole, it took about 20 to 25 minutes before the nurse who had gone to the laboratory was back in the ward.

This time seemed uneconomical when replanning the hospital, so it was decided to install a pneumatic postal system to transport the samples to the laboratory and send the findings back to the ward.

Just a few weeks after the new clinic was opened, the accomplished changes proved not to be having the desired rationalising effect. Sick leave amongst the laboratory staff increased, seemingly without explanation, and the quality of the laboratory performance sank. During the following months, the situation became more dramatic. In cases of emergency, time delays occurred which endangered the appropriate care of the patients. At the end of the first year after the clinic was opened, a great fluctuation was established amongst the laboratory staff. An inquiry amongst those who had handed in their notice revealed that, from their point of view, the introduction of the pneumatic postal system constituted the difference that made a difference between a well functioning and a badly functioning laboratory department. Whilst before, the laboratory staff had rated the working atmosphere both in the clinic in general and in the laboratory in particular as good and job satisfaction as high, these ratings were now reversed.

However, not only the clinic and the laboratory were now described differently. The employees also described and rated themselves and their roles differently. Before they had been important and felt that they were in a direct relationship with the patients' care. Even if they did not know or only rarely knew the patients personally, they did know something about them. Above all, they had an idea why the required tests were necessary and what value their own work had for the patients and all those involved in treating them.

The fundamental change connected with the introduction of the pneumatic postal system was obviously not the acceleration of the transport of blood and urine samples, but an intervention in much more complex regulating mechanisms: the possibilities for interaction and communication between the wards and the laboratory. This change in the organisational structure of the clinic led to a change in the laboratory assistants' construction of reality, i. e. their view of the clinic, the laboratory and themselves, which had far-reaching consequences.

This is an example of the fact that the planners did not fully realise the ambiguity of human behaviour, the short- and long-term relationship between means and end, for the nurses on the one hand and for the whole organisation of the hospital on the other, and so did not bear it in mind sufficiently.

On the level of exchange of behaviour, the nurses and the laboratory assistants were carrying out a satisfying transaction for themselves respectively. Among themselves they exchanged cigarettes and a light, friendship, mutual attention, gossip about the staff and the patients. For them this was the irreplaceable aim of the ritualised morning visit to the laboratory. The superficial organisational aim, transporting blood, was merely the means to an end and formal legitimation for means as well as end. Nevertheless, in the original arrangement, the organisation still got its money's worth. It received an activity necessary for survival (not just the transport of blood, but also the necessary extremely expert and fast laboratory work) in exchange, a fair transaction whose prerequisite was a special kind of combination of the activities of different people.

The organisation as a whole functions as long as this mutual "means to an end"-relationship between the organisation and its individual employees establishes itself. If this does not succeed or if the profit is too one-sided (to the advantage or disadvantage of the organisation/to the advantage or disadvantage of the employees) then, as in the above example, the life-ensuring environment is also questioned.

It is thus unavoidable to inform oneself explicitly as to what kind of payment is necessary to buy the employees' nontriviality, or in the sense of our radical market economy model: in what currency each individual does his accounting.

Every employee of an organisation is an observer who makes distinctions, attributes them a name (e. g. "working", "managing", "organising") and a value (e. g. "good", "bad", "efficient", "pleasant", "fervent", "profitable" etc.). Thus far organisation is always a result of human communication, an event that occurs in the heads of the participants.

Line organisation, line-and-staff organisation, multiple line organisation, matrix organisation, tensor organisation; functional structure, regional structure, field or product structure; centralisation, decentralisation; formal, informal; delegation, integration; structure, course; horizontal, vertical; structures, processes, rules, regulations, instructions, evaluating procedures, organisational instruments, models, organigrams ... etc.: all these terms float through the minds of managers and through the corridors of office blocks, are whispered in factory canteens with understanding or lack of understanding and discussed in seminars on economics. But what do these distinctions in the field of language, these boxes and arrows on flipchart paper have to do with what happens in an enterprise, with the recipes according to which you cook and then eat?

They are attempts to describe experiences, to learn a lesson from successful or unsuccessful organisation and remember it. But whose experiences can be described in this kind of language? Do the distinctions made in these models for the description of successful organisation correspond with the distinctions of those who (should) produce this behaviour? Do the cause-and-effect relationships construed in this way – from the outer perspective – include the relevant correlations between end and means for the enterprise as a whole system as well as for the employees? Can one deduce instructions for everyday actions – the inner perspective – from them? Matrix organisation, staff-and-line organisation: How do you do it? And above all: What purpose does it actually serve?

In all organisational models there is a risk of mistaking the menu for the meal, i. e. to make the mistake of believing the name of a thing to be the thing, the attributes of language and its terms to be attributes of what they name, the cook's name to be a recipe.

THE EVOLUTION OF ORGANISATIONAL PATTERNS —
AN EXPERIMENT

The developmental principles of organisations, the crystallisation of structures and the difficulties of changing them can best be illustrated by an experiment which can be carried out as an imaginary experiment, if necessary.

Ingredients for the following task

Take a group of people (10–20 persons) and a ball. Now set the following task for the participants:

Each person must say a number with three digits and each person has the task of remembering as many numbers as possible and the respective member of the group. When everyone has said his number, one member of the group throws the ball to another and calls out the recipient's number. If it is the wrong number, the recipient refuses to accept the ball and sends it back to the sender. If it is the right number, the recipient keeps the ball and throws it in turn, calling out the assumed number of another member of the group and so on.

Record of such an experiment

First of all the sequence of numbers was as follows: 974, 167, 853, 385, 425, 333, 439, 672, 333, 167, 539, 218, 999, 167, 911, 873, 111, 112, 333, 167, 999, 743, 629, 218, 167, 124, 333, 111, 999, 167, 218, 333 …

After a few minutes, certain numbers start recurring: 333, 218, 999, 111, 167 …, others are mentioned once or twice at the beginning, some never. Which numbers these are is determined by chance and necessity. The necessity is given by the participants' pressure to act. Each person must throw the ball if he wants to play. To this end he needs a recipient, i. e. he must remember the number of at least one other player so as not to miss the boat. As observer and player, it is easiest for him to remember numbers that somehow stand out from the mass of other numbers and capture his attention. On the one hand, this can be caused by the unmistakeable peculiarity of the numbers (111, 333 and 999 are "objective" as a result of their regularity, i. e. very conspicuous for every player). On the other hand, a more or less individual and personal attribution of meaning to a number can lead to a focussing of attention: 218 (the number of the German paragraph on abortion), 911 (model number of one's own Porsche) etc; or both coincide, the objective characteristics of the number and subjective attribution of meaning: 333 (the Battle of Issus).

In addition, other factors play a role, too: the history of the game and the relationships between the players. Every time a number is called the probability that the recipient is thrown the ball again increases. His address, his name is called back to the minds of all other players. The sooner a number is brought into the game (e. g. 167 in this case), the greater the chance. This is an example for the well-known principle of Matthew: For unto everyone that hath shall be given, but from him that hath not shall be taken away even that which he hath.[7] Something similar is valid for the importance granted the individual players by the others. The probability that a prominent personality's number is remembered is greater than that of someone the others consider an "underdog".

The structure of the game, the ever recurring pattern of interaction (who throws the ball to whom) is thus determined both by general and individual factors: by the given rules and prohibitions, the history of the game and the focussing of the other players' attention, which is mainly determined by their individual allocation of meanings. A regular pattern has ensued from the interaction of nontrivial machines.

This game models the processes in the development of organisational patterns so well because it entails all relevant elements of an organisation. For the players, their behaviour is the means to an end – they do not want to be out of the game. For this reason, they adhere to the given rules; rules telling them what they definitely have to do (pass the ball on and call out a number) and prohibitions telling them what they must not do at all cost (accept the ball if the number is wrong). This results in interaction between two persons

7 See also the explanations of the scientific sociologist Robert K. Merton, who proves this principle as far as scientific research is concerned, whereby an often quoted author is quoted more and more often and called upon to publish ever more, and an unknown one is never quoted and has problems publishing his work; R. K. Merton (1965): On the Shoulders of Giants. A Shandean Postscript. New York (Free Press).

which can be compared to the conclusion of a contract. The first player offers a commodity (plays the ball, calls out a number), the second accepts the offer (keeps the ball and plays on), the exchange is a success; or he declines the offer (returns the ball), the exchange has failed. Language and action must be linked in a special way. Anyone who throws the ball to another and calls out the right number, stays in the game. The pattern that ensues in this way cannot be controlled by any single person. Even an innovative player who remembers all the numbers of all participants cannot guarantee in the long run that a number sponsored by him is included by the others. He can call it himself as often as possible, but if this number is consciously excluded by the other players he risks being excluded himself.

Another factor that makes interaction easier or more difficult becomes evident in this experiment. The given rules of this game allow throwing the ball to another person only on the one condition that one knows something about him ("his" number). Thus knowledge is assumed.

If after a while, when a rigid, ever recurring pattern has evolved, you ask the players to develop a new, different pattern come hell or high water, generally nothing new at all happens at first. Innovation is practically impossible within the old rules. Neither good will nor threats result in once forgotten numbers being remembered. Only the announcement that the players will be immured as during the election of the pope promotes a little creativity. One of the players questions the basic rule that a number must be called out and calls out the addressee's name and place of birth. As a rule, this breach of the basic framework then leads to an arbitrary succession of connections between throwing the ball and linguistic descriptions: religions, directions, parties or such like are called out. However, this does not give rise to a meaningful and predictable pattern for the others, the individual freedom of all participants is unlimited, what they say is a matter of whim, it is arbitrary and unforeseeable. It no longer makes any difference whether anything is said at all, there is not even a recognisable order in throwing the ball, since for the observer there are no compulsory signs and symbols for everyone which could be examined for regularity.

After a phase of chaos and anarchy, though, signs of fatigue generally appear, all or at least the majority of players share the desire to send up white smoke at last: We have a new order!

One of the players calls out his own number (the sender) when throwing the ball, others follow his example. The proposed rule implicit in this behaviour allows all participants to be included as possible addressees. You do not have to know anything about them. The patterns are no longer dependent on the characteristics of the reference numbers, but on personal preferences to bring one or another of the participants into the game. However, this is only the case for a group of people with an extensive mutual past history. Where this is not so, no limitations of the partners the ball is thrown to develop on a longer-term basis, there is still a lot of scope, an extension of the possibilities of interaction.

As in this experiment, it is always rules that increase or decrease the probability of the development of one or another organisational form, extend or restrict options. Organisational forms can never be decided on as a whole when an enterprise is structured and organised, but only rules, i. e. a limited framework within which the self-organisation of patterns of communication takes place.

RECIPES

— *Put enough "artists" at the side of "housewives" so that they don't suffocate, and put enough "housewives" at the side of artists so they don't starve.*

— *Ask yourself about formal regulations: What makes them possible, what prevents them? What is easier because of them, what is more difficult? What becomes more likely, what more improbable? Whom do they serve, whom do they harm? How did they arise, and how and why are they maintained?*

— *Imagine that all currently existing project groups, teams, meeting forms remain in existence indefinitely. So when you arrange organisational structures you think very carefully about how you are going to get rid of these structures again once the particular problem is solved, the job finished, the specific demand for coordination overcome. Keep your options open.*

- *Don't organise everything yourself, but create the general conditions so that the persons concerned can shape their cooperation themselves.*
- *Don't seek perfect organisation. You would end in chaos. Be content with structural data and expect your performance providers to manage business processes, but not positions. This saves the organisation department from arduously compiling handbooks that often lose their validity as soon as they are completed. On the other hand, you then lose an important index for the distinction of planned (written) and real organisation.*

4. Performance

THE EFFICACY OF "EFFICIENCY"

In nearly all areas of the economy we come across various kinds of efficiency and/or "performance" as omnipresent concepts: "Show us what you can do before you start making demands!", "Our employees are paid according to their performance", "Of the twelve employees in my group, three or four do the majority of the work", "As an executive it is your job to assess the performance of your employees!", "In comparison to German and Japanese industry, the efficiency of American industry increased during the nineties", "The efficiency of the capitalist economic system is superior to that of the communist planned economy", "We must start rewarding work again!" …

The universal applicability of the concepts of performance efficiency is linked to the fact that they are also an extremely nebulous,

---

1 K. E. Weick (1969): Social psychology of organising. Reading, MA (Addison-Wesley), p. 86.

soft concepts. Two definitions are mixed together in their meaning: efficiency in the sense of mechanics and efficiency or performance in the sense of business administration.

In mechanics, performance, or rather efficiency, refers to movement; it is defined as the product of power expended and distance covered per unit of time: (power x distance) / time. The greater the distance, the heavier the vehicle and the quicker the goal is reached, the greater the performance.

For the application of this mechanical working concept to human work, labour economics has coined the term "intensity": It is expressed as the speed and effort exerted in carrying out a task.

All this smacks of effort; the more I pant, the more I achieve; no pain, no gain. Humanity after the Fall, expulsion from Paradise, Puritan ethics; effort per se is good, the more the better. But all this is not necessarily an expression of economic thinking.

In economics, performance normally involves an input-output relationship. Performance is equated with efficiency, the quantified relationship between input and output. The smaller the input and the greater the output, the more efficiently a system works and the more productive it is.

The corresponding term used in labour economics is "efficacy". Efficacy expresses the quality of a person's method of working. It can be recognised by how quickly, briskly, self-controlled, steadily, unerringly, rhythmically and relaxed the work is done.

In this case, performance means clever calculation in the sense of continuous optimising: shrewdness, slenderness, with no superfluous weight, the judicious use of effort.

The evaluation of performance – this is where the outer perspective comes into it – is determined by the aims on which an observer measures it. A good example from the technical field is the efficiency of a combustion engine. As a rule, the energy input (consumption) in the form of fuel is related to the energy utilised as driving power. This value lies somewhere around 30 per cent for normal automobile engines. The remaining 70 per cent heats up the environment among other things (even in the summer). In the customary definition of the efficiency of an engine in horse-power, the waste heat and exhaust are not included in the calculation; they represent a difference that makes no difference, they are imagined away ...(at least in this construction of reality called "definition of performance").

The concepts of performance and efficiency have far-reaching consequences for interpersonal relationships. They legitimise processes of differentiation, the annulment and simultaneous confirmation of the demand for equality formulated during the French Revolution.[2] Performance provides the justification for the differences between otherwise equal people. In Napoleon's army, every soldier carried the field marshal's baton in his knapsack.

The popularity of the terms performance and efficiency in the economy says something for their usefulness. This is probably based on their ambiguity, which gives the user and the observer the opportunity to put those quantities in relation to each other as "input" and "output" – as cost and benefit in the sense of radical market economy – that this user and observer want to be related, and to exclude those they don't want to be part of the calculation.

Inclusion of new quantities in the calculation of efficiency changes the entire process for all concerned. If the environment (or its advocates) were able to have its consumption (wear and tear) taken into consideration as cost-effective input quantities (costs) in the firm's cash flow, this cash flow would – as everyone knows – radically change. It would then be necessary to change the rules of the economy game and to redefine the inner and outer boundaries of the respective "economic survival units".

When we apply the economic concept of performance, we always do so from the outer perspective, we distinguish between system and environment, input and output. It is always a more or less arbitrary distinction whose efficiency invariably depends on the aims it is intended to serve. For even aims are never "given", but are always the result of agreements and decisions. If several people who work together agree on a mutual reality construction of "performance", this establishes a number of rules toward which not only the evaluation and selection of the behaviour of individuals is oriented, but also the interaction of all participants, their exchange of behaviour.

2 P. Heintel (1989): Hierarchie und Projektorganisation. Klagenfurt (unpublished manuscript).

PARADOX –
PERFORMANCE IN A CORPORATE PLANNED ECONOMY

"Closed loop controlling – closed loop control – is a process whereby one variable, namely the variable to be controlled (controlled variable), is continuously monitored, compared with another variable, namely the command variable and, depending on the outcome of this comparison, influenced in such a manner as to bring about adaptation to the command variable. The sequence of action resulting in this way takes place in a closed circuit termed the control loop." (DIN [German Industrial Standard] 19226)

This control loop model generally provides the frame within which the concept of performance is used within a corporation. There are two aggregate elements: the performing organ (controlled system) and the controlling and directing organ (the control). An employee (or rather his behaviour) becomes the controlled system, the supervisor (his behaviour) becomes the control.

In this kind of model, the aim of an enterprise or a sector has the function of a command variable. The result of a performance evaluation or examination has the function of the controlled variable and a (new) agreed objective or agreed performance the function of a manipulated variable. By means of agreed objectives or agreed performance encompassing all hierarchical levels, a universal control model for the enterprise is developed. These models are most highly formalised in extremely differentiated "management-by-objectives" concepts.

So much for the theoretical background. In practice, this concept, seeming so rational on the menu level, frequently has very surprising consequences.

First example – Oil refining industry:

After a long phase of development and decision-making, an incentive-wage system outside the collective bargaining agreement was introduced in a German oil refining enterprise for all executives. The prerequisite for this was performance evaluation of each manager by his supervisor. To this end, a plan was drafted reflecting the firm's strategic, operative and behavioural performance objectives. Then every supervisor negotiated a binding agreement on performance goals for the coming business year with each subordinate manager. Based on this agreement, the performance of the manager and the organisational unit managed by him was then evaluated a year later through consultation. According to the result of this appraisal, the scope of his salary for the coming year was fixed.

The unexpected result: After the first year in which the new system was implemented, the personal performance of the managers during this period was evaluated on average as very good to good in the evaluation consultations, but simultaneously the sales trend of the enterprise stagnated in a way which could not be explained by external factors.

Second example – computer manufacturer:

Less spectacular but similarly unexpected is the experience of a computer manufacturer on introducing a sales-supporting laptop-software combination. Using the laptop and modem, the salesmen were able to retrieve or process information and make on-the-spot agreements during consultations with customers. Previously this was only possible over several appointments. The object of the investment was to take some of the load off the salesmen as far as administrative work and travelling was concerned, and give the salesmen more time for their real task, namely selling. In order to assess the efficiency of this procedure, it was also agreed to record the number of contacts made with customers and to use them as a performance criterium in the sense of a controlled variable.

An assessment after one year revealed a distinct increase in contacts with customers. However, and this was the highly unsettling and unpleasant surprise, the anticipated stimulation of real acquisition activities in the area of new customers failed to materialise at all because the salesmen contacted old, good contacts more often than before.

The problematical and unplanned side effects arose in both examples because all those involved in the project did exactly what was agreed on.

The paradoxical result can be explained with the help of the radical market economy model.

In the first example of the oil refinery, linking salary stipulations to agreed performance objectives created a profound change in the market situation within the enterprise for the behaviour of the managers concerned. In the past it was up to them and their supervisors to decide which behaviour should be considered as performance and when. In principle, they were able to draw on numerous possible activities. The new model, on the other hand, meant that for the period of one year, all possible behaviours that could receive the benefit of the distinction "performance objective with effect on salary" were listed beforehand. Two examples for this kind of performance objective are:

- initiative (independence in perceiving, taking over and carrying out necessary tasks, initiating and consistent pursuance of optimisation processes and new ideas)
- asserting cost leadership for polypropylene

The exchange conditions were fixed in a similar way. The new model fixed a formal quantitative correlation between the degree of realisation of a performance objective and the extent of the variable part of the salary in the following year. From the perspective of the managers, the commodity exchange processes thus initiated must have transpired approximately as follows: "Deliver five units of initiative plus eight units of asserting cost leadership for polypropylene for 3000 Euro variable parts of salary …"

Obviously the individual managers were extremely successful in managing the prescribed limited range of products and the newly fixed exchange conditions – measured against the excellent results of the performance assessments.

The market value of the product "achieve turnover" within the firm, which was obviously higher in the past, sank. On the other hand, the transactions made possible on the new market for the above-named products – initiative and assertion of cost leadership, for example – turned out to be so lucrative that it seemed appropriate to the managers concerned, all good businessmen, to put a new strategic marketing concept into practice as a result of their carefully performed market analysis. To express it a little less complexly: They did something that was worthwhile for themselves but no longer concurred with what was worthwhile for the enterprise.

A similar dynamic probably occurred for the computer manufacturer's salesmen in the second example. In this case, too, the traditional intercompany market began to shift as a result of the introduction of a new promotional electronic data processing system and/or new rules governing performance evaluation. For the old product "customer contacts", management signed an unlimited purchase guarantee. This deal seemed particularly lucrative because of the exchange value agreed on with the buyer for the period of one year, independent of demand. The fairly general product specification additionally enabled unlimited use of the cheap raw material "old customers".

The dynamics of the market revealed here can be characterised by the following features:

- The fixed value of a product supplied as a commodity enables an exchange between these commodities in accordance with previously known binding parities.
- For each product, the guaranteed amount purchased is fixed in accordance with defined conditions.
- Which product on a market can be exchanged for which at what amount and according to what parity is fixed.
- All these provisions are made by a central planning authority. These dynamics can be labelled most pertinently as exchange of commodities in accordance with "planned economy" rules.

    The social and economic risk potential connected with this is comparable to that of a planned economy. The simple control loop is a model that obviously does not do justice to the complexity of human relationships. Simply thinking in loops, then, does not suffice to save managers from failure. They have to be the "right" loops.

THE BLACK MARKET –
THE SELF-ORGANISATION OF UNPLANNED CONTROL STRUCTURES

In planned economy systems, black markets arise which paradoxically ensure the survival of the planned economy. This is also valid for intercompany planned economy as manifested in the presented performance evaluation systems oriented on the control loop. This is most obvious in the dynamics of piecework systems in the everyday life of a company.

Piecework is a certain form of incentive wage. The fundamental structure of piecework is simple: a certain amount of time is estimated for each process, the "normal time". This is the time it takes a person of normal skill under normal exertion.

Anyone who works normally for one hour gets a "cheque" for 60 minutes. Anyone who works faster gets 75 or 80 minutes on his cheque, for example. Thus in the primary loop, workers do not earn money but time, measured in the currency of "minutes". In this model the performance of workers can thus be calculated simply using the following formula:

Performance indicator Z = (given time / actual time) x 100 (%)

Assuming the cheque amounts to 75 minutes, the resulting performance indicator is: $(75 / 60)$ x $100 = 125$ %. So for this hour the worker receives 25 % more than the normal rate.

These time credits can be freely converted into money. The exchange rate is fixed by a joint contract or a company agreement, and so cannot be influenced by individuals. You get the money when you exchange the cheque, so-called "piece-rate tickets", in the wages office. Or you save them up as insurance against bad times.

The piece-rate system is planned consistently as defined by the economic performance context. Efficiency is the input-output relation. From the perspective of the production planner, the output of a workplace is the number of parts leaving it, input is the money value spent on it. On the one hand this depends on the number of minute cheques and on the other on the exchange rate money / minutes. The number of minute cheques is in turn dependent on the definition of normal time. This is determined in so-called time schedule catalogues. These catalogues are devised and maintained in another division: operations scheduling.

The lower the per minute costs – at constant number of parts –, the higher productivity. As long as the conversion factor does not change, the efficiency of the workplace is not affected. From the perspective of production planning, however, the advantage of working fast is obvious. The higher the performance indicator Z, the higher the plant's degree of utility.

Let us now change perspective and take a look at the job from the view of the worker. In this case the efficiency calculation seems quite different: minute cheques as output, exertion of effort, skill, experience and knowledge as input.

In the sense of the radical market economy model this once again describes dynamics that correspond to the mechanisms of an exchange of commodities in accordance with planned economy rules as described above:

– The fixed value for the commodity "skill and effort", which is defined by comparison to normal performance, facilitates exchange for the commodity "minutes" in accordance with previously established binding parities: every worker knows what he gets a "minute" for.

– Within a certain range there is even a company purchase guarantee for the amount of "skill and effort" employed. It usually lies between 85 and 48 standard minutes per hour, that is to say between 70 % and 140 %.

– As central authority, operations scheduling determines what behaviour (product) at a workplace can be exchanged for minute currency to what amount and according to what parity. This can be looked up in the time schedule catalogues.

As long as workers move within these planned economy rules, the transaction transpires as follows: The input of skill and effort produces parts. In exchange for this the worker gets the fixed quantity of minutes per part as credit on his cheque. Within a certain quantity range (guaranteed purchase), the output of minute currency per hour and thus the possible hourly wage can be increased or reduced in proportion to an increase or reduction in the input of skill and effort. In the long term this is not a satisfying result for a good businessman. The price for his own commodities is regulated, he cannot attain a higher price of his own accord. The result can only be improved if he succeeds in changing the exchange rate between the commodity supplied (skill and effort) and the units in minute currency he gets in exchange. In principle there are two ways to accomplish this:

1. By reducing the expenditure of skill and effort per part, provided – if the production process is simplified, for example –
it can be ensured that the determined minute currency per part
remains the same;
2. by declaring produced parts that are really bad parts as "good"
parts.

However, both these methods run counter to the interests of production planning and operations scheduling, so they cannot be realised
on the official "white market".

This realisation provides the start signal for a more or less bloom-
ing black market, depending on the enterprise. The most important
traders are workers, works counsellors, foremen and time-study men
from operations scheduling. With a lot of creativity, products are
developed, supplied and exchanged for other commodities contrived
just as creatively. These transactions could be carried out as follows:

Quality controllers control more generously and so get social
acknowledgement and respect from the producers, in the work place
as well as, and particularly, outside the company, and above all for
their families as well …

When a new machine requiring considerably less skill and effort – expenditure – is installed, a time-study man refrains from
changing the normal amount of time per part determined in the time
schedule catalogue. In exchange he gets less opposition from the
workers in his other activities …

A foreman is prepared to turn a blind eye to all these transactions. In exchange, a works' counsellor declares his willingness to
support him before the personnel manager in a personnel matter …
etc.

If you scratch my back I'll scratch yours. Control loops are not
only planned, they also arise spontaneously and organise themselves.

What is special about these examples is that they are nothing
special. Production managers could tell you a thing or two about
that. Where markets are controlled by central authorities as planned
economies, black markets flourish. This makes everyday transactions
enjoyable again and prevents the threatening monotony. New behaviours (commodities) can be developed, bargaining is possible,
cartels can be formed, price fixing agreed …

Considerable amounts of the commodities "skill and effort" are taken away from the "white market". Trading them on the black market is a lot more lucrative. From the outer perspective of industrial management this means a considerable loss of productivity.

However, that is nothing special, as the following example shows: The scene of the plot is a paper factory. In the course of the manufacturing process the rolls of paper obtained as output of the paper machines pass through a so-called calender. The calender's function is to smooth the surface of the paper. This is achieved by running the webs of paper through a number of rolls positioned one behind the other. The paper is pressed together and compressed repeatedly between these rolls. This smoothes the surface. At the end of the process, the single webs of paper are rewound. In the next step they are cut, packed and then dispatched. A web of paper has to pass through the calender until the required smoothness has been a-chieved. The machine operator determines when this is. In order to test the smoothness, he puts his hand on the web of paper coming out. If the paper is not smooth enough, the customers complain: The paper is not suitable for printing or rather the printing quality is bad.

Too much smoothness means less profit because the paper is put through the calender needlessly. The considerable cost resulting from this is not compensated for by the customers.

Accordingly, to be a machine operator on the calender is quite a responsible function, so only reliable and experienced paper makers are put on this job.

In the course of extensive technical investments, the scenario is fundamentally changed, similar to the example of the computer manufacturer. An electronic device to measure smoothness is installed on the line. An integrated measuring sensor registers the smoothness of the paper as it slides past and compares it with the set target value. When the actual smoothness reaches the target value, an acoustic signal sounds. In accordance with the instructions given him by production management, the machine operator now stops the machine. It is his job to lift the smoothed roll out of the machine, put it down, insert a new roll and start the process over again. This means that it is no longer the machine operator's job to test the smoothness.

However, one of the machine operators cannot refrain from testing the indicated smoothness by putting his hand on the paper. Surprisingly enough, he often finds that in his estimation, the target value has not yet been reached when the measuring device gives the signal. The measuring device obviously makes mistakes. As he has clear and unambiguous instructions to rely on this device, though, he informs the shift overseer every time. And each time he is told to stop checking the measuring device and accept the indicated values.

So now the machine operator gives himself a secret task. He adheres strictly to the instructions of the measuring device, but carefully notes down the batch number of the rolls for which he assumes faulty measurements and compares these numbers with those for which complaints come in. The higher his private quota of hits, the more satisfied he is with himself, his personal performance and his job. However, this does not alter the fact that for months, rejects are produced constantly, although (or because) shift overseer and machine operator conscientiously fulfil their agreed tasks.

From the radical market economy point of view, in this case a technical investment and the new definition of the tasks of the machine operator connected with it have resulted in a profound disturbance of his personal market. The new instructions mean nothing other than a planned economy intervention that forbids him from dealing with the product "testing smoothness". The machine operator's assortment of commodities is to be limited to "monitoring the machine", "switching machine on and off", "inserting and taking out paper roll". This limited supply no longer enables the machine operator to achieve satisfying results on his personal market.

The expenditure side of his business account could no longer be balanced by appropriate proceeds. More or less by chance he discovered the possibility of realising a demand (his own) for a new product, "prognosis of faulty measurements by the measuring device", on the black market.

In such a radical market economy you can even be your own business partner, your own customer. Our machine operator succeeded in exchanging his product "prognosis ..." for considerable amounts of "interest in his own work" and "self-esteem" of the finest quality. He could even bear the loss in value of his official "white" business account which occurred during the transfer of profits made on the black market. In this way he was able to balance the current business year satisfactorily.

The analysis of this example gives rise to a few consequences worth thinking about – not only for piecework or the use of machinery, but also for the managing activity of managers.

All performance models and all procedures of performance evaluation involve descriptions made by observers. Supervisors, planners and managers make distinctions from the position of the external observer, make designations and perform the evaluations they consider relevant. This is always accompanied by the risk of mistaking "menu" phenomena for the "meal" or even for "cooking". This is always the case when different distinctions are made on the level of designation and evaluation to those made on the level of behaviour, i. e. when what is (positively) evaluated is not done.

As far as the models presented here are concerned, the first difference between these two areas of phenomena lies in the dimension of timing. Yearly periods usually form the basis for procedures of performance evaluation. The agreements refer both to the targeted objectives of an enterprise or sector (e. g. cost management) and to the targeted behaviour of managers and their employees (e. g. finding widespread consent for important decisions) which ought to be achieved within one year.

The more formal, precise and effective the agreed objectives are, the more improbable it is that alternative objectives emerging during the year will be perceived and added to the catalogue of objectives. This makes it impossible to react with the speed appropriate to changes in the environment; the manoeuvrability of the enterprise or sector is forfeited. In spite of repeated warnings, the Titanic, which was actually still manoeuvrable at the time, did not accept as an obstacle the fact that an iceberg was emerging in a part of the ocean in which – according to the knowledge and experience of the captain and the first mate – there had been no icebergs so far. Collision and sinking were the result.

The potential risks of closed description and evaluation systems (control loops) evident in the examples point to another correlation. In these examples it is not a case of being closed to the external environment of the market, but to the inner environment of the employee. Employees always endeavour – from the radical market economy view – to make attractive business deals. The less this is possible in the frame of agreements construed according to a planned economy, the more attractive and determining black markets become. The desire of the persons controlled to use the rules of a control system as an incentive for individual, profitable bartering must not be underestimated.

Recipes

– *As soon as you have succeeded in calling something "performance" in an acknowledging fashion you can do business with it unhesitatingly. No transaction is easier to legitimise than giving someone money for his performance.*
– *Define the desired performance as casually and vaguely as possible. The usefulness of the term performance lies to a great extent in its unclear and manifold meaning. The more detailed and complete the targeted objectives that you fix for yourself, your employees or for organisational units alike, the more risk there is for your firm if all concerned really adhere strictly to these agreements.*
– *Leave the choice of means to an end open! If you don't, you increase the risks arising from too clear target objectives tremendously.*
– *Show your employees whether they have achieved a lot or little in your opinion, but without telling them how they did, or did not, do it. Your conclusions in reference to money and career will be accepted. However, absolute precision is called for when you are asked why something you call an objective or a performance is an objective or a performance for you.*

5. Leadership

> "Where conflicting opinions are concerned,
> anyone who appeals to authority
> is working with his memory rather than with his mind."
> Leonardo da Vinci[1]

> "The tigers show us how far we can go and
> we show the tigers how far they can go."
> Siegfrid and Roy[2]

GENERALS WITHOUT SOLDIERS –
THE PECULIAR MILITARY METAPHORS OF MANAGEMENT

Among the images and comparisons chosen to describe the activities of managers, warlike metaphors are particularly popular. These range from "strategic" planning, "staff" and "line" in an organisation to the "fight" for market shares and the director "general". The fact that such picturesque language prevailed for such a long time implies that it seems appropriate and suitable to its users. It obviously complies with managers' experiences. However, it might also be the case – this is one of the peculiarities and idiosyncrasies of human language – that this kind of experience is not the cause but the effect of the tacit equating of economy and war chosen here. What we want to think about now is whether it is practical and useful in the everyday life of a manager – in particular for his tasks of leadership – to

1 Quoted in W. O. Steinhardt (1985): Toskana für Liebhaber. Berlin (Arcus) p. 118.
2 Statement by Siegfrid and Roy, two wild animal tamers from Las Vegas, in the German television programme "Wetten, dass ...", 14. September 1990. At October 3, 2003 the tiger Montecore showed Roy that he went too far.

see the market as a battleground, the enterprise as an army and his employees as soldiers.

Let us begin with the behaviour expected of soldiers or forbidden them in the organisation of an army. There are few other forms of organisation that try to realise the ideal of the trivial machine to the same extent as the military (possibly youth sects, strict religious orders and revolutionary parties' cadre forges; it is no coincidence that these bring forth party "soldiers" or the soldiers of some promised Kingdom of Heaven).

Even basic training begins by making externally controlled automatons of autonomous bodies whose movements are controlled internally: "Halt, eyes right, forward march, right wheel!" The behaviour of the individual is standardised and adapted to a whole procedure which follows, or at least ought to follow, clear and predictable input-output (i. e. order-obedience) mechanisms.

The relationship between a leader and his followers is based on a clear and unambiguous division between those persons (groups, units) making the decisions and those carrying them out, between the subject and the object of the decision. Prerequisite for such a hierarchical form of leadership is the functioning of the organisation or its sub-units in accordance with a clear cause-and-effect formula. A superior's decision, his instruction or order is the cause for the behaviour of subordinates (the individual soldier, the company, division, army etc.). The individual soldier, various military subdivisions and the military as a whole are instruments in the hands of technicians who apply the rules of mechanics.

In the army, a lot of time and energy is spent on converting this mechanical ideal into reality. Soldiers are "drilled", refusal to obey orders is severely punished, in war with the death sentence. Thinking (= nontrivial behaviour) is not desired – the lower the individual's position in the hierarchy, the less desirable it is; any deviation, any stepping out of line is a disturbance and is sanctioned. "Leader, give your orders, we will follow you!" is the fitting and desired internal view of the recipient of an order (or its analogy: "The Party is always right!"). Maintaining these organisational rules seems just as important as – if not even more important than – winning battles, at least in peace time. For only if the whole apparatus functions in this centralised way, it is argued, is one prepared for an emergency.

As this kind of structure has survived in most of the world's armies, this type of leadership and organisation seems to conform adequately to their specific objectives – military clashes. However, this does not mean that it is also valid for successful economic activities. Centralistic, planned economy models with the most similarity to military structures are obsolete, i. e. they do not survive and are doomed to extinction like the dinosaurs (there is no international protection of species agreement for this field).

Rigid order and hierarchical structures such as those established in this exemplary manner by the military prove their functionability whenever decisions need to be made and acted on quickly. When only a commander-in-chief has the say, he still has enough to do weighing up the pros and cons of his decisions, but he can rely on and refer to his own, more or less logically self-contained background of experience, his knowledge and values. He is not obliged to clarify and elucidate his objectives, assumptions and the background of his decisions over and over again. The less people are involved in the process of decision-making, the less time is required to find a common language, to work out the premises of the respective suggestions, settle conflicting values and aims etc.

Wherever quick actions and short-term reactions are imperative for survival, rapid decisions and short channels for carrying them out are essential. If a fire breaks out, it is better not to convene a general meeting of the occupants of the house, but to call the fire department, since they know what to do without long discussion. If a ship is sinking, a responsible captain can ensure the passengers' safety by ordering a quick and well coordinated (= organised) action. Where surgical operations are concerned, it is usually recommendable to let the surgeon decide what needs to be done. Wherever pressure of time is involved, hierarchy is a reliable form of coordinating the behaviour of a number of people. This is probably the reason why the military has preserved its structure for so long. In an emergency there is always time pressure. And the time between emergencies allows for training for emergencies, it is not a reason to change the organisation – not even for those condemned to the role of receiving orders.

This is the only explanation for the fact that so many people allow themselves to be forced into a soldier's uniform and sell their nontriviality temporarily in such an extreme manner. But the credit they receive for this on their credit and debit account is generally not only material but also non-material: their own honour and that of their native country, protection of the Western culture from the threatening Huns from the East, service for God and the King, preserving their own life and property and that of their relatives and loved-ones, their wives, children, parents and lovers. All this and much more can be credited to individual accounts or rather, should they desert or refuse to do military service, be registered on their own accounts or those of their fellow men as minus. So the majority obey the supposed factual constraints and, controlled from within and with seeing eyes, enter a situation in which they must be controlled from the outside. They obey because it seems to be a good deal or because the alternative looks like an even worse deal.

However, would they do it if no outside pressure forced them to? Can you compare an enterprise with the fire department or an army? Can a manager lead like the captain of a sinking ship or a general in the field? What would constitute an emergency? What would be the time in between? Or is there always war? But above all, do the employees, in the role of the soldier, experience the situation as war, too, so that they would be prepared to relinquish their nontriviality, i. e. their autonomy, interior control and freedom relatively cheaply? And if they were, would that really be an advantage for the enterprise?

At first sight, the idea that one could "conquer" a market in the battle for market shares and "win over" competitors' customers seems to confirm military mechanical thinking once again. Battles are always about gaining extra space, controlling a certain territory. The same seems to apply to markets. The European market is "dominated" by the Germans and the French, the American market "taken by storm" by the Japanese, while California industries are constantly trying to "occupy" the region of the Pacific. Nevertheless, there is a difference between gaining territory in the wars of the history of our times and asserting a product on a market. First of all, victory only gains land for the military; war as a real estate transaction by means of which unproductive capital is accumulated. For control over territory by no means ensures anything useful resulting from it. At best it can prevent anything happening that the conquerors don't like. An occupied country is usually inhabited by people who do not allow their behaviour to be controlled. You can promise them bad deals if they manifest undesired behaviour ("Anyone who makes rebellious speeches in public will be shot!"), but you can hardly force them to love their victors. In the extreme, the product of military conquest is deathly quiet, passivity. What matters in winning market shares is not the territory gained, but the activities of the customers exclusively. They, as autonomous living beings, must make the decision to buy. They have to be satisfied so that they make similar decisions over and over again, tell others of their decisions, spread enthusiasm etc.

Herein lies the significant difference between an enterprise and an army. The military serves to avoid or suppress undesired behaviour. Disturbances of or threats to a desired and valued order have to be removed, the supposed enemies rendered harmless. Thus far, then, it seems to be correct that military representatives constantly maintain that it is their job to prevent war. Insofar as they devote themselves to defence they belong to those who do housewifery in a country.

Enterprises, on the other hand, cannot be satisfied with coping with emergency situations and warding off trouble-makers. A market is a living system which can only be maintained as long as someone is there to ensure that it is maintained. When no-one buys anymore, the market is dead. Constant, ever recurring activities of the buyers, the production of a particular behaviour by the participants in this market process are necessary. Products must be developed, produced and supplied, buyers have to be found, sales contracts concluded, payments effected etc. It is a question of making cooperation possible, for trading with others is cooperation.

Even in relationships with competitors, the war metaphor seems to have limited use, as in the long term the elimination of competition, gaining monopoly, can have fatal effects on an enterprise (just think of the monopoly of the German Democratic Republic's car factories on their market). Monopoly can make you stupid and security can lead you to bankruptcy.[3]

3   More about this later in the chapter on "Planning".

In the long term, the use of the military metaphor as intercompany philosophy proves its limitations for the practitioner. He may well believe that there is always war, but most of his employees just won't go. The more qualified they are, the less they will agree to such a world view. Their enterprise is not their native country, they can change it – even if this is not always easy. And if the enterprise should really go under, the competition will receive them with open arms together with their loved ones, and maybe even give them a better salary. For them it is never really a question of the alternative "all or nothing", "fight" or "go under", "life" or "death". They have a choice, they can obey or not obey.

So the problem is deciding for which sectors of an enterprise and in which times a hierarchical organisation is useful and where and when it is more likely to cause harm. Although it is a question of the survival of divisions, enterprises and markets – living systems –, we nevertheless do not want to go so far as to recommend executives in the economic sector to orient their style of management to the top performance of gardeners rather than to that of generals.

POWER –
WHO WANTS WHAT FROM WHOM?

The idea of power guiding our everyday thoughts is largely connected with the cause-and-effect-model. The one who has power (an object?) determines what happens to those who are exposed or subjected to this power.

From the view of systems theory and constructivism, this kind of interpretation of power that is ascribed to a person as an attribute or possession, is far too simple. Living beings are in correlation with each other. They mutually determine their living conditions and influence one another, and yet the behaviour of an individual is never completely controlled from the outside. However, when the degree to which this mutual influencing is possible is not equal for all the participants, it seems reasonable to speak of a relationship of power. From the perspective of an outside observer, the person with power in a relationship is always the one who can restrict or extend the behavioural options of his partner to a greater extent than vice versa.

Or, to put it in terms of radical market economy: The one with power is always the one who has the greatest influence on the exchange rate for behaviour.

People, and other living beings, cannot control and predict each other in the sense of the trivial machine, but they can reduce the unpredictability of their fellow men by preventing undesired behaviour, i. e. by limiting scope of behaviour. You can throw political opponents and sex fiends into prison, an instrument of power, in order to prevent them from political agitation or from sexually molesting little boys and girls. Force is, then, one of the poles in exercising power. Military power is the classic example, criminal law another. The threat of death for someone who does something he should not do (murder, for example) is the extreme form of this kind of exercise of power – limitation of behavioural options.

On the level of social rules, it corresponds to the commandment: "You shall not ...!" Seen from the viewpoint of radical market economy that means: "If you do not put a certain refrainment on the market, or rather if you supply a certain product (behaviour) not desired by your business partners, you will get a commodity in exchange that you probably won't like either, as far as anyone can judge (punishment). Measured in your own currency, you will be making a bad deal!"

The opposite of this form of power resulting in passivity is enticement. In exchange for a desired behaviour (an activity) you are promised a good deal: "If you supply a behaviour I desire, I will offer you something it would be difficult for you to get otherwise!" The promise of an incentive trip to Mexico, a little cottage in the country, a numbered account in Switzerland, of a career, honour and glory is an example for the fact that correlations between people can be designed in such a way that one opens up options to the other that would not normally have been available to him. As an autonomous business partner he then has the choice of whether to deliver the desired commodity or not. On the level of rules of the game, such promises are linked with commands following the pattern: "Do this and that ...!"

Thus power is not a question of cause-and-effect relationships, but of good and bad business transactions under varying market

91

conditions. For the framework of the market – the context, i. e. external reality or what the participants take for it – determines to what extent one can extend or decrease the options of the other.

In our case the question is always: Who wants what from whom? Or even: Who wants more from the other person, who is more dependent on whom under the given conditions at the present time? Or: How do the participants see the current situation and their own scope for concluding better or worse business transactions with the other, or who is in a position to say no?

From the point of view of longer term, more satisfactory business relationships, it is always better to make sure that no-one feels cheated, and certainly not if he has the choice of exchanging his commodities somewhere else. If you see an enterprise as a market and management as transactions with activities following the laws of market economy, you should choose the second form of exercising power – enticement – if you want a certain behaviour from your employees. If you prefer the first form, you will inevitably promote passivity and practise selection under your employees, which will only leave those who have no alternative.

However, enticement only succeeds when you supply something that attracts the person you want to entice, i. e. something valuable or enjoyable. The prerequisite for this is to know (or suspect) what the other person would like to "buy". The better an executive manages to put himself into the position of his employees, the easier the following assessment will be: How can I, in competition with other enticements, focus attention on my offers, transform the hesitance and coyness of my employees into a "yes" and into actions?

- You are the only one I can entrust with this task.
- He must finally have noticed how good I am in comparison with the others.

Leading = Misleading

Fig. 11

At this point we would like to introduce another thought experiment:

Imagine a marketplace or – less idyllic – an international trade fair. You have a few stalls there, too: the career stall, the stall for an incentive wage, the stall at which you can be patted on the shoulder, another for confidential talks, one for projects. On the other hand, the competition is also quite well represented: Husbands or wives and lovers present their offers, the president of the tennis club has put up placards on independent alternative careers, children extol their shining eyes and happy smiles …

Now three of your employees come into view. Will you manage to be seen by them, to involve them in a longish sales talk, sell (exchange) your products without having to reduce the price and be so convincing in all this that the buyers do free advertising for you?

COMPLEXITY –
THE MANAGER'S MANY MARKETS

"Divide and conquer!" was a reliable strategy of leadership even in the Rome of olden days. It is admittedly questionable whether – as the term "strategy" implies – there is really always planful intent behind it, or whether it is merely an attempt to reduce the complexity of interaction, which increases immensely as soon as more than two partners are involved. For all relationships of exchange and power described so far can best be analysed when only two partners have to agree on their relationship and their transactions.

A manager's life only becomes really difficult and complicated when he provides several customers with a commodity simultaneously and receives services in return with which he doesn't always reckon and that he doesn't always like. His behaviour is put into frames of interpretation and evaluated by different people; and then he is paid (back) in accordance with their accounting with an "appropriate" behaviour.

An example:

After a series of quality cycles in his sector, a production manager realises that part of the difficulties in producing consistent quality can be traced back to the fact that sales concludes ambiguous contracts with customers and plans ahead far too late. At the sector manager's meeting (where he has to speak) he has to listen to such reproaches as: he represents only the production shift, lets the foremen influence him too much and has absolutely no understanding of the market (he is a "traitor" to enterprise orientation).

After successful consultations with the area managers, this production manager now informs his foremen – not without pride – of the following results: "The present market situation is characterised by ever shorter planning cycles and customers pressing for ever more punctual delivery, so it is only possible to plan in two-day rhythms. For this reason we must coordinate more closely with Sales and Stores. As part of this coordination we will also come to an agreement on misleading quality criteria!"

Pride is followed by annoyance when the foremen comment on this form of problem solution as follows: "So production counts for nothing any more?!", "Sales always gets a good deal!", "Does anyone still represent our interests?" Once again he is the traitor, this time to the "cause" and the "party" of production.

As a member of diverse groups, the very structural situation means that a negotiator who acts successfully and flexibly will always somehow be part traitor and double agent. Taking our radical market economy model as a basis, we can say that successful managers have to supply many markets, practise market research and product development in them, take care of customer relationships and lead price negotiations. In this sense, employees are to be regarded as customers. The business field of managers is characterised by the specialty of manifold linkage and interdependencies. This makes it not exactly easy to manage the business and tempts one all too often to demand too much of oneself and to do too much. The capacities of one-man/one-woman business set limits to these efforts, and this has absolutely no effect on the market situation as a whole.

Another example:
The employees of a textile store, who have so far arranged displays in their shop windows with great success, and have thus "produced" the decision on the goods to be presented in the window display on their own, become agitated and peeved when they are supposed to buy these goods from their new manager. As this enterprise has a hierarchic organisation, they have no choice but to buy the goods "manager's decision" in accordance with their "obligation to purchase". However, the manager does not recognise his original ideas in their presentation. He did not take into consideration what he was going to get in return.

And while he keeps struggling on this barely attractive market it escapes his notice that in the meantime his customer "Board of Directors" has acquired the commodity "ideas on a new location policy" from another competitor (the manager) and paid for it with appreciation, further steps in his career and admission to the strategy team of the enterprise as a whole.

MAGIC –
HOW LANGUAGE CREATES REALITY

Bride and bridegroom stand before the altar – two free people with no ties. Then the priest says the formula: "I now declare you husband and wife!" Now they are lost, both have changed their identity from one second to the next, they are no longer the same, they are man and wife, pay their taxes differently, their rights and responsibilities have suddenly changed, sometimes their names, too etc. And how? By means of a magic formula – pure magic!

The marriage ritual is just one impressive example for the magic creative power of language in human coexistence. Life in enterprises and institutions is also determined to a considerable extent by such symbolic acts. Promotions and transfers are pronounced, top-bottom relationships are defined, business objectives proclaimed, fusions carried out. Where before, a normal, nameless employee of the firm sat at a standard desk loaded with files, there now sits a member of the Board in solitary splendour behind a splendidly shining, completely empty mahogany table that makes an observer want to play table tennis. Where before two equal colleagues sat together at lunch, a boss and his subordinate are suddenly eating together.

Language is the medium in which the coordination of human behaviour mainly takes place. There are, of course, quite a number of nonverbal ways to communicate – from mimicry through gesture and intonation to significant silence. However, all these ways of exchanging information are far more ambiguous than that of language (which is ambiguous, too, but the scope of interpretation is limited to a certain extent).

Thus through language, magic plays the key role in human organisation: It ensures that all the autonomous individual beings are linked together. With its help, rules of interaction are established and maintained.

On examining which linguistic forms regulate interaction between colleagues in the offices of California enterprises, three distinguishable forms were found: announcements, orders, and promises.[4]

With these three kinds of linguistic communication, you can find all the prerequisites for a game following radical market economy rules. Rules of the game, as already stated above, consist of just such descriptive and prescriptive rules.[5]

---

4   T. Winograd a. F. Flores (1986): Understanding Computers and Cognition. Norwood, NJ (Ablex) p. 143-162.

5   Cf. G. H. von Wright (1963): Norm and Action. A Logical Inquiry. London (Routledge & Kegan). And F. B. Simon (1988/93): Unterschiede, die Unterschiede machen. Frankfurt a. Main (Suhrkamp).

To control the game of "Enterprise", these three forms of linguistic communication are obviously sufficient to supply the necessary descriptions and instructions for acting. Announcements establish the generally binding aspects of the enterprise's reality (for example: The works holidays begin on 15 July! As from now Mr. Maier will take over the management of the Sales division). These announcements serve to attribute identities and roles and, in connection, define the relationship in reference to who has anything to say to whom. Orders and promises supply the raw material for the development of prescriptive rules (in accordance with the free market economy). An order opens up the exchange transaction, it is comparable to a classified ad under the "Wanted" section, it is – quite literally – a demand ("Bring me the Synet Chicago file, please!"). With the promise a price is named – oriented toward the future – which will be offered to the exchange partner for satisfying the demand ("Sometime you will get a rise, be promoted etc.!").

However, communication by means of orders and promises is not one-sided, from top to bottom, but mutual. Even formal subordinates demand certain behaviours from their supervisors and promise certain services in exchange.

Whenever supply and demand meet together, there is always a market. The difference between the business partners consists in the difference in their power, i. e. in the options open to both partners: How prices are negotiated depends on which of them wants more from the other. This does not always have to be the one who is formally the supervisor.

However, management is affected by the magic of language in yet another sense. As soon as someone is transferred to a management position (by announcement), he is no longer the same person he was before, neither within the frame of meaning "enterprise" nor in external representation. All at once all his behaviour is interpreted as management behaviour. In the evaluation of all concerned, this gives it a new meaning, a different (probably higher) exchange value.

A few examples:

The same sentence heard after a three-week holiday, "Nice to see you back!" triggers completely different reactions depending on who says it and when: Your secretary, to express her delight, or your own

97

boss a few minutes later to indirectly communicate his disapproval at your long absence.

An older foreman who has been promoted and works in the training division opens a seminar for younger colleagues in the following manner: "And in the evening you can have a drink." What he really wanted to say was that the firm was paying the bill. Yet since the enterprise was going through an economic crunch at the time, the seminar participants interpreted the statement of their superior ill-humouredly as a ban on drinking more than one beer.

The new director general of a conglomerate wants (a) to change the style of interaction between "top" and "bottom" and (b) to find out the opinions of the "plant". To this end he goes to the canteen, joins the queue in front of the serving counter with a tray and finally sits down at a table. He chats informally with his neighbours, a conversation between colleagues. He is close to achieving objective (b). In order to realise objective (a) as well, he introduces himself affably: "I am the new director general!" All at once the whole situation changes. There is no more informal chatting; the new director general only hears what is intended for members of the board of directors; the conversation between colleagues is over.

When you have been identified as a "manager" you cannot not manage. Whatever you say or do will be understood in the sense of an order, an announcement or a promise (in the negative sense: a threat). Management is a game, so we can conclude, in which the magical effect of orders, promises and announcements is utilised. A transaction that not only includes real values, but calculates with the shadow of the future – a transaction with options.

WITCHCRAFT –
THE MANAGER, INSIDE AND OUTSIDE AT THE SAME TIME

The market, the enterprise, the division, any form of organisation can be regarded as systems that consist of linked behaviours. However, they can and must also be seen as environments for each other, whose stability has to be protected for its own survival. In this complicated network of systems and environments, what role does the manager play in his leadership function? For he is obviously not an element of all these systems (he is not his behaviour, he merely produces it). Nevertheless his behaviour does have something to do with these systems and environments, it preserves and can change their form.

At this point it is worthwhile to take recourse to the military metaphor (although the metaphor of the gardener would probably lead to the same conclusions). Why is it that in former times commanders used to prefer to take up their position on a hill? The answer clarifies a little what leadership functions are all about: Because as an observer you have a different overall view from this raised position than down in the tumult of battle. The view from above opens up the perspective of the external observer. One of the advantages of the American General Schwarzkopf in the Gulf War was that reconnaissance satellites helped him to obtain an unsurpassable picture of the situation. What could be seen from this position "from the outside" could be utilised for action "on the inside". Someone with access to information from the neutral bird's-eye view recognises connections that remain hidden in the organisational blindness of the inner perspective. This opens the chance for dissociated, sober and rational analysis, for strategic and ecological thinking: system and environment can be set in relation. The task of a manager is essentially that of alternating between both perspectives, keeping an eye on the various environments of his enterprise (the market as well as the psyche of his employees), simultaneously being trainer and player in his team, and referee as well – all of these, and not just one, absolutely biased and yet completely neutral. He falls between two stools, as they say in German, or rather he is sitting on the fence.

Management is witchcraft. At least the metaphor of the witch best catches being inside and outside simultaneously, the mediation of two different positions of observation. For the concept of the witch originally meant "someone who sits on the fence".[6] If we content ourselves at first with this superficial definition of location of the manager position, he actually has to sit on two fences: the fence separating players and spectators (i. e. the participating and acting observers on the field and the non-participating and non-acting observ-

---

6   The German word for witch, *Hexe*, derives from the old high German *hagzissa* or *hagazusa*, whereby *hag* means fence. Cf. F. Kluge (1883): Etymologisches Wörterbuch der deutschen Sprache. Berlin (de Gruyter), 21st edition 1975, p. 307. (Translator's note: The Anglo Saxon for witch is similar, *haegtes*.)

ers on the bleachers); and the fence separating time past and time future. He must also always stand with one foot in a hypothetical future world and anticipate what might be in store. This requires a sense of possibility,[7] the imagination to enable him to imagine what risks and chances await him and his enterprise (in particular when these are never completely predictable).

In the Middle Ages, witches were burned at the stake because (really or supposedly) they did not fit in with the generally binding belief and behaviour system of their time. They challenged unshakable truths, and as herb women they quite pragmatically used traditional century-old experiential knowledge for their art of healing, which ran counter to orthodox teachings. They applied special methods of treating living systems which did not fit the thinking of their times and their environment. This threatened the established hierarchy, which was based on knowledge by propagation, on a higher authority outside this world.

This is the very task of a manager, however: Not to content himself with the certainty of truths that cannot be analysed, but to doubt obvious presumptions and dogmas and soberly analyse the relationship between the organisation for which and in which he is responsible and its environment, together with all its contradictions. Only if he continuously questions the obvious constructions of reality in the enterprise can he broaden his scope of action and that of his enterprise and utilise it optimally.

The opposite of this is cutting out all information that might disturb wishful thinking and self-confidence. It is the Erich-Honecker or the Berlin Wall syndrome: the victory of the calming, blinkered inner perspective over the outer perspective. It is easiest to achieve this when you surround yourself exclusively with employees who only ever say what you want to hear (an illness unfortunately not seldom found amongst managers) and when you – to close the loop – only give your employees information that will pacify them and confirm their world view.

The decisive prerequisite for utilising the outer perspective is radical neutrality, a view freed of all wishful thinking and all bias, as far as possible. Only someone who examines all imaginable connec-

---

7   Cf. R. Musil (1930–1952): The Man without Qualities. New York (Knopf), 1995.

tions between single factors and variables without prejudice can come to conclusions which were not obvious up till now. This person can also see how often the decisions and actions within an organisation bring about paradoxical effects: Good intentions are only too often the opposite of "good". If the network of very diverse variables is not grasped, you cannot calculate with the consequences of decisions, often very far from your mind as far as time and space are concerned.

An example to illustrate this:
The supervisor of a customer-related division of a bank is faced with the problem of holiday scheduling for the summer. All six employees are experts, four have to be there to guarantee trouble-free work processes in the division. There are overlaps in the dates desired by the six employees. Each of them has good reasons why he has to go on holiday at this time and not at any other. The supervisor tries hard to find a just solution, weighs up one's reasons against the other's, supports one employee (sick child) and tries to make the other (luxury trip) understand … He comes neither to a satisfactory solution for all concerned, nor are his pains acknowledged by the employees. On the contrary, they are all annoyed. For some he was too hesitant, for the others too ruthless etc. Had he held on to his neutral, outer position without declaring his position regarding content, and merely moderated the decision-making process of the six employees of the division by focussing their attention on the consequences of the various alternative solutions, the employees would have recognised how complex the problem was, explained their mutual priorities and values and kept the responsibility for finding an adequate solution. As team members, they would not only have been able to experience their respective inner perspective, but also to utilise the view from the outer perspective.

From this neutral position of observation, not only do regular correlations become observable which increase the probability of achieving maximum results with minimum effort, but also such regularities which continuously lead to the very opposite of the aspired objective being achieved. Living systems constantly organise themselves in such a way as to balance opposite tendencies. Anyone who, bound up in the inner perspective, concentrates all his energy on steering such a system in a certain direction will inevitably activate counterforces that present themselves as resistance, insubordination and sabotage. On the other hand, if he puts himself on the other side of the scales, he can be certain of activating forces which will then counteract these tendencies. "Managing" always means juggling – the art of witchcraft.

MOTHER AND EXECUTIONER – THE PERSONNEL DIVISION AS TRIVIALISER

When managers are given the (hypothetical) alternative of either occupying themselves more with factual professional questions and less with personnel matters for the same salary, or less with factual professional questions and more with personnel matters, three out of four managers choose the task of a qualified professional.

Apparently managers seem to find the notion very tempting of no longer having to keep struggling with other people, of being free from disputes over holiday schedules, of no longer having to look into discontent faces at the distribution of awards, never having to keep an eye on, motivate or control anyone else etc., in brief not having to manage anyone any more.

Someone who has to deal with the already often mentioned soft reality of human relationships and the non-triviality of human individuals every day, inevitably develops an almost insatiable longing for the predictability and security of trivial machines. The hard reality of factual questions in which there are clear data and formulas to determine what is right and what is wrong promises a simple life following the rules of logic in which, as a manager, one knows what one must do or can at least find out by using one's brain.

However, in organisations in which the behaviour of people has to be coordinated, communicating about factual contents and relationships at the same time cannot be avoided, come what may.[8] To put it in radical market economy terms: You always supply several commodities simultaneously. Even if you intend to offer a behaviour for exchange which gets its value from factual and professional reasons, you are still always supplying a commodity that is assessed for

8 Cf. P. Watzlawick, J. H. Beavin, D. D. Jackson (1967): Pragmatics of Human Communication. New York (Norton).

its meaning for intrahuman relationships. And you are the recipient of the appropriate service in return.

So what should you do if you can only achieve your professional objectives at the price of occupying yourself with this softer relationship reality? In organisations there is a reliable method not open to individuals: division of labour. One ideal on which this is based (even if it is not always realised) is the split between these two markets, the division of responsibilities and competence for professional questions on the one hand and for "relationship services" on the other.

This involves delegating the task of seeing to this softer area of reality and ensuring that it becomes harder to the personnel division and its employees. This is another prime example of collaboration, of teamwork, in which a mutual conflict is divided between two parties. The conflict between the ideal of the predictability of human beings on the one hand, and the fact of their unpredictability on the other, is eliminated by the specialists feeling mainly responsible for professional necessities and the personnel people for the relationship dimension of the joint task.

In this polarisation each participant helps the other to maintain a world view relatively free of ambivalence. If the personnel division's employees did not see to …, the employees of the … -division would have to do it themselves (and vice versa). This division of roles reminds us vaguely of the traditional clichés of the division into men's and women's roles within the family. The man develops and takes over competence for factual questions (which car to buy, how to invest money, how it is earned etc.). The woman does relationship work and devotes herself to taking care of emotional and human needs (she practises the personal development of the children and ensures triviality, i. e. smooth functioning, the household).

Now we do not intend to suggest a new metaphor for describing enterprises ("We are all just one big family"), but rather to point out how certain life-preserving functions are safeguarded in the frame of division of labour within organisations. From the outer perspective the cooperation of those who undertake these tasks becomes clear, even if it remains undiscovered from the inner perspective of the participants.

The work of personnel divisions is thus a good example for the paradox of housewifery in organisations (in enterprises as in families): The better it functions, the less its necessity is noticed. In all probability, as in other administrative sectors, the personnel division within your enterprise which is acknowledged will be the one that is not completely successful. If it were successful, it would probably be quite simply forgotten.

When children behave badly, it always reflects on the parents (as everybody knows!). Something analogous applies to the employees in the personnel division. They are the mothers, the professional scape-goats, who can be beaten and heaped with reproaches when there are problems with or among the personnel. And it is they to whom desires for provision and demands are directed.

"How on earth did XY get the job?" is one of the most frequent questions, even if the relevant employee has already been in the firm for 15 years. The personnel division is the door to the enterprise, this is where you enter the life of the enterprise. It is here that the magical formulas are said which seal the birth of a new employee and turn an applicant into an employee.

"I'd pay you more, you know how much I value your work, but the personnel manager is obstinate!" In a similar way salary systems are cursed which are usually attributed to the personnel manager, they are his "children". In the struggle for redistribution of scarce goods (money, holidays, prestige), the personnel division always presents itself as the external enemy that can be used to keep relationships harmonious and free of conflict.

It is probably no coincidence that a lot of company kitchens are assigned to the personnel division. In earlier times you went to the wages office to collect your money. In times of cashfree payments the nutritious aspect of the organisation needs a different symbol.

"We really need career planning!" is a further demand, and on the quiet it is said (or at least thought): "I don't want anyone meddling in my own decisions." A number of similar conflicting feelings are involved. The desire for welfare and the fear of one's own freedom being limited represent the two sides of the same coin.

Besides this, the power of the personnel division is imagined as being very great: It is the personnel division that guards the records, only the personnel chief knows how much everyone earns. And for some, it is an open question whether he also knows who goes to the rest-room how often, who drinks how much alcohol on the job and who takes company pencils home illegally … In times of increasing computerisation, these justified worries are on the increase. It is easy to find out who plays which video games on which company computer, as well as who phones his aunt when. "Big Brother" sees everything. The personnel chief as omnipotent observer, director of a secret service who misses nothing and forgets nothing.

Moreover, it is he who, as executioner, takes over the execution, who flings an employee out of the life of the company. He is the executioner who, based on division of labour, has to put the decisions of others into practice.

Besides these ordering functions, personnel divisions of larger enterprises have increasingly taken on other tasks that frequently conflict with their ordering functions: that of internal advisors.

Although they are biased co-players, they have to take on the role of external and neutral observers, trainers, coaches or specialists for personnel development, management development, training and further training, performance evaluation, salary systems, work organisation etc.

This role of a player who pretends to be an outsider often leads to problems of self-reference. The salary system that would be best for the enterprise must not necessarily be best for the advisor, and vice-versa. A contradiction develops between the currencies in which the performance of such an internal advisor is evaluated. For the enterprise, for example, it is of paramount importance to give bigger rewards to persons in direct contact with customers and who thus have a direct effect on turnover. If we assume more or less constant personnel costs – or rather a constant relation to profit contribution – then internal areas such as the personnel division have to stand back. Awards are then reduced for this sector, increases postponed: all unpleasant consequences for those occupied in this sector. The paradoxical effect on the internal advisor is that his factually good advisory performance (commodity) means a money-losing operation for himself.

It is thus not surprising – again for reasons of reducing complexity and eliminating contradiction – that in this sector the division of labour within organisations is restructured in favour of division of labour between organisations. The internal advisory divisions of large enterprises are disincorporated. They create an image for themselves as independent firms on the advisory market. And as a counter-move, the enterprises buy the advisory performance they need on this market. This cancels out the blending of the distinction between inside and outside which creates paradox.

At this point the loop to the theme of management closes again. In the longer term, even the internal splitting of competencies between the factual and relationship level of communication and organisation will probably become invalid. Wherever people are affected by decisions, it will be the task of managers to consider and carry the consequences. If you think you can produce human organisations without human beings, you succumb to a fiction in which what is fundamental and characteristic is "imagined away". To bring it to a point: A manager can manage without factual and expert competence, but not without competence on the level of relationships.

RECIPES

- *Practise witchcraft and sit on the fence between inside and outside: Alter your perspective now and then and observe your enterprise, your division and yourself from the outside – soberly, critically, neither flatteringly nor pessimistically. What kind of relationships do the respective units you observe have with your environments, i. e. other enterprises or divisions, colleagues and employees, customers and competitors? If you do this regularly, you have a relatively big chance of preventing organisational blindness.*
- *Try to entice instead of forcing. Put attractive offers on the behaviour market, negotiate fair prices.*
- *Regard your employees as economically reasonable, good businessmen (or women) with whom you can only stay in business on the long term if their accounts are satisfactory, too, i. e. when profit and effort (give and take) are balanced according to their internal analysis sheet.*
- *Sell special, attractive products, not mass-produced goods, i. e. don't do what all the other managers in your field do! (E. g. when everyone offers open doors, it might get draughty, but whether this alone leads to communication is open – like the doors.) Note: Products are subject to a life cycle – examine your institutionalised meetings, for example, to find out which phase of their life cycle these are in.*

- *If your attempts to motivate fail, hypothetically give yourself the blame, for once. In this way you will be able to act again. Ask yourself which of the behaviours you supply are exchanged over and over again for disinclination to work, lack of creativity and lack of initiative. What has become inflationary? Admonitions, praise, eternal promises? What new commodities could you put on offer?*
- *If you are a manager always remember: Whatever you do as a person in the context of the firm or in your private life but within view of colleagues, employees, supervisors – it will be perceived as the actions of a manager. (Even your offer "Let's put the boss to the side for a moment" is the boss's offer). Your behaviour is a commodity with an exchange value on which you get feedback through the behaviour of others. (Some things you are given back, others are "paid back").*

6. Planning

> *"To plan is to bother about the best method*
> *of accomplishing an accidental result."*
> Ambrose Bierce[1]

> *"A great climber of this world said,*
> *you get furthest when you don't know*
> *where the path goes."*
> Johann Wolfgang Goethe[2]

WEATHERMEN AND RAINMAKERS –
THE SOFT REALITY OF THE ECONOMY

It's the same as the weather: Forecasts are never exact, frequently inaccurate and sometimes not right at all. If you take your umbrella with you the sun shines, if you only put T-shirts in your suitcase the outdoor temperature sinks to freezing.

On the other hand, anyone who thinks that the sun is shining because he has an umbrella with him would be accused of magical thinking. Weather seems to develop independent of what we do. We, the victims of a cold front from Scandinavia, are the ones who can only react, and not the culprits, the rain "makers". A frog in a jar, to use the German metaphor, shows us whether the weather will be nice tomorrow, but it cannot bring us a high from the Azores by climbing up its ladder. At least, that is the natural, everyday world

---

1   A. Bierce (1946), quoted in K. E. Weick (1969): Social Psychology of Organising. Reading, MA (Addison-Wesley).
2   J. W. Goethe, quoted in R. Friedenthal (1963): Goethe – Sein Leben und seine Zeit. Munich (Piper) p. 291.

view in our Western culture. In other cultures in which the distinction between people and their physical environment, between subject and object, cause and effect is not as rigid as ours, the possibility of influencing the weather is rated much higher. For the North American Indians, rainmakers are highly renowned personalities (which probably speaks for the fact that they were/are successful).

Meanwhile mathematical models exist showing that the development of the weather is influenced by the slightest changes. If a butterfly flutters its wings in Vienna today, this can result in a thunder storm in Tokyo two months later. The world is a highly complex system full of correlations. However, this philosophical insight is of little help where taking up the profession of a rainmaker is concerned, for the influence of the butterfly effect can be reconstructed in retrospect, but it cannot be used to produce thunder storms. The weather does not react like a trivial machine. We cannot describe definite input-output correlations, i. e. there are no definite dancing steps or rhythms for producing drizzle.

The situation of the economy is similar, although the butterfly effect is far more lucid. Forecasts change the weather, market research changes the market. This applies to the "big" market in which material products or services are traded, as well as for the "little" market in which individuals exchange behaviour in their dealings with one another.

Whilst the weather forecast deals with the relatively "hard" data of physics (atmospheric pressure etc.), the economy - seen from the radical market economy perspective this applies to all interaction between people – is dealing with one of the "softest" areas of reality. If we measure the difference between "softer" and "harder" reality by the extent to which aspects of reality are altered by the fact that they are being observed[3], this can certainly be established for markets. It is always observers (buyers and sellers) who distinguish between different commodities – whether automobiles or behaviour –, give them a name, assess them and finally buy and sell them. This is how a market – self-organised – develops. If the descriptions and evaluations of these observers change, the market changes: a prime example of soft reality.

3 See F. B. Simon (1990): My Psychosis, My Bicycle and I. Northvale, NJ (Aronson) 1996.

Planning in the economic sector, or generally speaking within human relationships, runs up against a fundamental difficulty. It has no clearly separate object that it can study and for which it could make forecasts. Planning is self-referential, i. e. a part of the processes of observation making up the market. It is these processes of observation that planning professes to study and plan. Thus planning must always take into consideration that planning occurs and that this may possibly change its own prerequisites. All this, however, not only applies to planning processes in enterprises, but also to personal planning by individuals. From the perspective of radical market economy, the following remarks on the planning and strategies of enterprises can also be applied to the situation of every single individual.

Planning must always take into consideration that in economic processes it is not so much a question of factual decisions as of the effects of the observations of observers observing observers during observation.

FROM "STRATEGIC PLANNING" TO "EVOLUTIONARY PLANNING"

Central control is not possible for living systems and their environments. However, the fact that we constantly run up against the problems and limits of planning in the economic sector ought not entice us to the deceptive opinion that we can do without planning. Quite the contrary. If observation is able to change reality, it needs to be planned. But it is not as simple as the planning an engineer does when building a house; he can rely on the bricks not suddenly reacting with fear and consuming no mortar in order to stay mobile in bad times and not get involved in unnecessary bonds. Planning must take the fundamental logic of processes of observation into consideration and reflect on which distinctions, descriptions and evaluations are undertaken.

"Strategic planning" and its most important element "strategic marketing" are the key words that currently stand for enterprise planning. Even they seem to follow the dubious military metaphor: the competitor as the enemy, marketing as war, planning as strategy. Here, too, the questions already posed above arise once more: What happens after the victory? Is peace only conceivable in times of monopoly? And if this is the case, how long can it last in a living world that is beyond any kind of one-sided control and regulation?

Let's replace the term "strategic planning" by "evolutionary planning". This should not only account for the fact that the development and survival of an enterprise cannot only be threatened by the victory of competitors, but also by changes in the environment, and that the dynamics of survival, growth and prosperity of an enterprise are more likely to follow the principles of selection and change described in the theory of evolution than (merely) the rules of war. In biological processes of evolution, the unit of survival is never only a species or genus, but always species or genus plus an environment in which these are able to survive. The same principle applies to enterprises. As a unit of survival, the enterprise should never be considered on its own, but always as the enterprise together with its various environments (markets, employees etc.). Without these environments the enterprise cannot survive either.

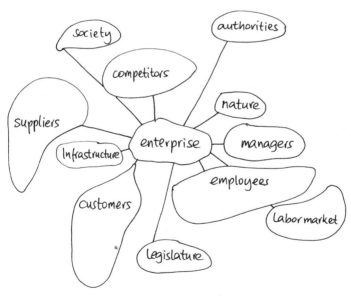

Unit of survival = enterprise in its environment

Fig. 12

In this respect, planning serves to cope with the complexity arising from an unforeseeable number of factors in the correlations between enterprise and market. The observer can no longer dissociate and distinguish the effects of these different factors. The danger of any description of such complex connections lies in the fact that they are either simplified too much or too little. If they are simplified too much (example: interaction as a closed circuit) then the model does not register all relevant factors for the behaviour of the system and its environment. The resulting overall view and the impression that these factors can be planned are deceptive. If they are not simplified enough, a model ensues which is so complex in itself that no overall view can be gained from it.

The change in the demands made on planning in the last decades reflects what varying aspects of the system-environment-relationship (enterprise-market-relationship) were considered important. Thus after the Second World War, the primary characteristic of a successful strategy was ensuring the long-term success of the enterprise. At this time, when production was a priority, the near future was predictable to a certain extent. The massive demands of the market had to be satisfied. The order of the day was to reduce costs as far as possible and to establish rationally functioning organisational units with the highest possible level of division of labour. This is a relatively "hard" area of reality, so planning could be accomplished on a relatively pragmatic level.

As the markets then developed more and more to buyer's markets (in the early sixties the principle "The customer is king" asserted itself) and the idea of marketing arose, the increase of an enterprise's flexibility emerged as a second planning requirement.

The organisational answer to this was the establishment of smaller, more flexible organisational units – for example the beginning of project management in its more limited form. This was the time of market priority. The area with which planning was occupied became "softer", for the market could not be fashioned autonomously – or at least not to the same extent as production. "Market observation" was invented, that was the magic word, and thus this observation of set actions changed the market.

In recent times, even the priority of the market has begun to topple. The increasing complexity of the buyers' needs and the impossibility of clearly limiting target markets has led to an ever greater and inestimable variety of products.

The connected trend away from the principle of quantity resulted in very different planning requirements. Not only was the control of large units now central to production, but above all modular serial construction, assembly in smallest units, production "just in time". The path from central mass production to decentralised production for customers rendered it necessary to adopt an individual quality demand in production and market planning. The manager therefore had to submit increasingly to the priority of communication if he wanted to satisfy these often contradicting demands.

Thus a supplier of trucks, who was proud of his quality standards, lost a big share of the market in South America because he defined quality only in terms of his own internal standards and not according to those of the South American buyers. Technological trifles such as ABS were not nearly as important for them as the possibility of driving through potholes at high speeds.

A manager only has a chance to realise the third general demand of a successful strategy, namely utilising synergy potential, by respecting the high status of communication within the company, between companies and outside the company.

It is quite fascinating to have the opportunity of seeing problems developing or "produced" within an organisation not merely as stress or even as a threat to another part of the same organisation, but as a resource and as a chance to utilise synergy effects. However, the prerequisite for this is communication structures enabling analysis of the positive and useful sides of the problem.

Thus a big Austrian industrial enterprise, for example, used the problematic situation of the waste it produced not only to develop new procedures of waste disposal, but also to sell this technology and the services connected with it to others. And a technology conglomerate used difficulties occurring within the organisation to establish and qualify an organisational development team that also supplies its services on the external market.

All these planning requirements serve an evolutionary goal: the survival of the enterprise. To a great extent, planning difficulties result from the fact that – contrary to a widespread misunderstand-

113

ing – in evolutionary processes it is not the "fittest" who survive, but survival is proof of fitness. So there is not just one way or one best way to survive, but many that "fit".[4] Because of this we cannot objectively clarify which decisions need to be made. Instead, as we have mentioned before, there is a lot of truth in the statement that many roads lead to Rome and there are always a number of options (or in this case means of transport), each connected with varying advantages and disadvantages.

Planning thus requires weighing up, persistence and reflection. In order to deal effectively with the danger of a too great or too small reduction of complexity, it is generally advisable to have planning done by groups in which as many of the potentially relevant factors for the development of the enterprise are represented, whether they are located within or outside the organisation, whether they are elements of the system or the environment. It is a question of organising conflicts and uncertainties, of allowing the views of participants with various goal definitions and inner perspectives to clash. Seen from the outer perspective, this is the only way to increase the probability that a widespread but inevitably limited expertise is used optimally and that the environmental conditions are taken into consideration adequately. It would, for example, probably be very useful economically to make a professional environmentalist a member of a planning group in the chemical industry. Conflicts in such groups are not disturbing, but necessary. Going beyond the limits of the evaluation standards of individuals, this is the only way to negotiate which data is definitely important, possibly important, or absolutely unimportant; and in the long term this is the only way to avoid the Erich-Honecker syndrome, an observation only ever confirming one's own wishes and presumptions.

Participants in this kind of planning process must thus be able to withstand a great amount of uncertainty, ambiguity, contradiction and conflict. This is easier for them if they know that none of the individual perspectives can claim to be the only truth. For breaking down perspectives and the discussions connected both with this and

---

4 See E. von Glasersfeld (1981): Introduction to Radical Constructivism. In: P. Watzlawick (Ed.): The Invented Reality. New York (Norton) 1984.

with putting them back together again are the result of teamwork under division of labour. This enables all participants to play the role of advocate for their individual reality and values without too much ambivalence. We are talking about one of the "collaborations" already described above, in which both sides of a mutual conflict are divided between two or more persons, whereby each takes one side of his conflict off the other's shoulders.

This function of reducing ambivalence becomes particularly clear when one person tries to weigh the argumentation of this kind of process on his own. The conflict dynamics of the group are then transferred to the one who devotes himself to such a task. Sooner or later he develops a feeling of being inwardly torn.

It is important to differentiate between planning processes and operative measures which can be controlled sensibly by unambiguous and clear functional structures (day-to-day business, routine functions, emergency situations etc.). In order to realise tactical considerations, matrix-like structures are suitable in which conflict potentials produced in the matrix nodes can be handled sensibly. Strategic planning with an evolutionary character demands fixed procedures and self-reflection, something that inevitably requires a lot of time.

The chances of such reflective group processes lie in preventing individual persons turning a blind eye to things and, closely connected with this, delaying and avoiding non-functional activities. Refraining from doing things is a commodity, too, and its exchange value becomes clearest in careful reflection. This form of planning is the counterpart to an emergency situation in which decisions need to be made promptly. Both tasks necessitate different organisational structures and should not be mixed. From the radical market economy point of view, these are two different markets in which good business transactions can be made, but with very different commodities. Hierarchically organised and prompt planning can be just as fatal as sticking to all the procedural elements of decision-making processes when someone needs to have his appendix taken out or when a ship is sinking.

THE POSITIVE POWER OF "NEGATIVE" THINKING –
THE CONDITIONS OF DYING AND THE LIMITS OF SURVIVAL

The relationship between living systems and their environments is not direct and causal.[5] Changes in the market are never the "cause" of a certain effect on the side of the enterprise. That is, there are always a number of different possible answers to market fluctuations and transformations. Living systems and their environment(s) are in a relationship of mutual limitation of options. The interaction between system and environment determines which structures and behaviours of a living system are impossible or rather incompatible with survival, i. e. it determines the conditions of dying (out).

A person's physical make-up together with the conditions of his physical environment determine that he can only survive for a few minutes under water without technical aids (it takes his breath away) or has to pay for a jump off the Empire State Building with the dissolution of his bodily organisation (in contrast to a dove). But in no way can either gravity or the chemical and physical nature of water influence deterministically (in the sense of a cause) what a person has to do. They merely limit his options.

The same applies to the relationship between an enterprise and its environment. The only really "hard" data available as a basis for planning are the conditions for the death of the enterprise.

The first step of any planning process consists in becoming aware of the limits to survival. In this it is recommendable to use the positive force of "negative" thinking and systematically work out suicide strategies. What is the quickest, easiest, most elegant, most excruciating, most shameful, most tragic, funniest, most exhilarating way to destroy the enterprise, division, sector, yourself? What do you have to do to achieve this and what ought you refrain from doing? The answers to these obviously rather absurd questions demonstrate the tacit prerequisites of survival quickly and drastically.

---

5 See also Humberto Maturana who presents in detail that there is no "instructive interaction" between a living system and its environment, i.e. changes in the environment merely effect a "perturbation" to which such a system reacts in accordance with its own structure – it is thus always interaction between the conditions of the system and the environment; H. Maturana (1976): Biology of Language: The Epistemology of Reality. In: G. Miller and E. Lenneberg (eds.): Psychology and Biology of Language and Thought. New York (Academic Press).

What are the minimal demands that guarantee survival – at least after a fashion? What kinds of behaviour need to be furnished at the very least? What organisational prerequisites does this necessitate? In the same way as a human organism has to eat, drink and breathe, the survival of an enterprise is linked with certain activities; the punishment for refraining from these is death.

On the other side of the spectrum, the life (or survival) sphere is determined by what is possible at the maximum. What would you have to do to be absolutely certain of the firm going bankrupt, being taken over etc.? So what kind of activities must definitely be refrained from if you want to guarantee its survival?

This method of "planning boundaries" attempts to answer the question "How do I prevent failure?" before the question "How do I achieve a goal?". This ought always be the beginning of any analysis. In a specific case it may be sensible to establish that the increase in turnover should not be less than three per cent and not over 15 per cent (since otherwise considerable changes would have to be made in production capacity).

To carry it to extremes, a hypothetical bankruptcy, gone through during planning, helps to prevent real bankruptcy as it marks out the scope and freedom for business activities. This kind of thought experiment focuses the attention of all participants on a mutual goal, in spite of all heterogeneous interim objectives, namely to minimise the probability of the enterprise dying out. For the enterprise is means to an end for the employee's (division's, sector's) own survival, it is an environment that their egoism demands should be maintained. This is the best way to activate the forces of self-organisation and mutual utilisation of resources and to lessen the tendency to hinder and sabotage each other.

Establishing concrete objectives always has a normative influence and limits options; establishing the limits of survival, on the other hand, opens up scope for the creative development of new options.

A GOOD ANSWER, BUT WHAT IS THE QUESTION? – ENTERPRISE, PRODUCT AND BUYER

You cannot kiss a market. Even a market is merely a figment of our imagination, an abstraction, something we cannot perceive with our

117

five senses. It is always problematic to include circumstances and things that do not exist in planning. On the market, enterprises are not dealing with things and matters, but with customers, buyers, potential buyers and others with whom they have to start communicating.

It is a question of the decisions of individuals to buy or not to buy the products of individual enterprises, and the decisions of individual enterprises to supply or not to supply certain products etc. However, the participants' decisions are not made independently from each other, they are not coincidental, but rather related to each other and influence each other mutually. That is what we call "market".

The most fitting metaphor to enable us to grasp the most significant characteristics of this process of mutual influence is that of conversation or dialogue. On the market, goods and money are exchanged in the same way as sounds, words and sentences in conversation. They are commodities connecting the enterprise and the buyers ("structural coupling"). They are the means of communication, bearers of meaning. The fundamental axiom of Radical Market Economy can be reversed here: Commodities, too, are means of communication ascribed different meanings and values ("use") by different observers.

For the buyer, an automobile can simply be a means of transportation, a status symbol, proof of creditability or potency, a means to self-realisation and a certain self-esteem (and a lot of other things). For the manufacturer, it is a commodity whose sale ensures the existence of the enterprise, enables expansion etc. Any product can become a sign of identity for the buyer and the seller. A man/woman of the world drives, wears, eats, drinks ..., men who wear braces/ women in pinafores drive, wear, eat, drink ..., conservative people consume this ..., progressive people that ..., young people, on the other hand, ..., grannies and grandpas ... But for enterprises, too, this is connected with ascribing properties and character, shaping an image, the development of an identity.

If we look at the relationship between seller and buyer under the aspect of communication, every product is both question and answer at the same time, depending on the perspective from which we observe it. The supply of a product on the market is (more or less unspoken) connected with a series of questions to the potential customer: "Do you want this? Can you use it? What does owning this commodity mean to you, what use is it and how much is it worth to you? Who or what are you when you own this commodity?" Such questions always have a suggestive quality. However, the supplied product is also an answer to the customer's question/demand: "Where can I get …? Who can supply what I need in order to …? Who can make me what I want to be?" Products are often answers to questions not yet posed. These answers also have a suggestive effect. They direct attention to the question belonging to it, they promote the invention of questions/demand.

This mutual, suggestive relationship between the communicating partners, sellers and buyers, must thus be the centre of planning and the product must be analysed as initiator of relationships and bearer of meaning. Conversation, this mutual twisting and turning[6] is generally not limited to two participants. Lots of different parties are involved in this question and answer game, cooperating and competing in many various ways in order to get into conversation with each other or to disturb the dialogue.

So there are four areas involved in "evolutionary planning":

a) The area of products: Which products are supplied on the market by the enterprise, which are demanded by the customers?

b) The area of the enterprise: What meaning and what value does selling these products have for the enterprise? What picture of oneself and others, what image, what corporate identity results from the spectrum of product range, its composition, the quantity and quality of the products sold, and the characteristics of a typical buyer in the eyes of the public? But above all, what role does it play in the economic survival of the enterprise?

c) The area of the customer: What meaning and what value does the acquisition of these products have for the customer? What picture of himself and others, what image, what identity re-

6 "Conversation" derives from the Latin *convertere* "to associate with, to come and go".

119

sults for him from buying these products from this supplier? How big is the circle of interested parties, what are their characteristics? What role does acquisition of this product play in the economic survival of the customer?

d) The area of the relationship between enterprise and customer: Who wants what from whom? How is power divided, i. e. who needs whom most? How exclusive (monopolistic) are both sides in relationship to each other? How big is the market niche, the scope of survival in which the enterprise has to eke out an existence? Amongst how many competitive suppliers and offers can the customer choose?

These areas form an unity. That means they have to be considered as linked together in a circular fashion. They mutually influence and limit each other. In the final analysis it makes no difference where we start planning on this merry-go-round, where we start the cycle. The decision should be made according to utilitarian considerations. When planning the construction of a new enterprise, you have different options and degrees of freedom (choice of products, target group, desired identity etc.) than when planning for a long existing firm with a traditional range of products and a public image already established over decades.

Let us begin with the identity of the enterprise. As a first step to establishing the actual state, it is sensible to keep to a neutral external perspective that includes all conceivable viewpoints. This is the only way to register the circular relationship between the attribution of meaning to products by the consumers on the one hand (the external market), and by the employees of the enterprise on the other (the internal market). What does it mean for the buyer of a certain automobile make if the manufacturer also makes washing machines – and missiles? What does this mean for the way the employees see themselves and for their identification with the firm's objectives?

The second step is then a definition of the enterprise's objectives. What should the difference be between the actual state and the target state and when? How would you notice this difference, that the objective has been realised, in the sectors – enterprise, product, buyer? But above all, would the identity of the enterprise be guaranteed when this objective was realised, or rather would the desired identity be realised? Should a difference be achieved at all, or just the actual state secured? What external changes and challenges need to be taken into account in such a case?

These feed-back loops can be seen between all factors of import for evolutionary planning. Enterprise objectives and identity can get into a mutually negative relationship ("If the desired objectives are achieved, identity is lost", or vice versa: "If the desired identity is realised, the objectives cannot be achieved"). The same applies to products and objectives, identity and products, and – not mentioned so far – the operative measures selected to achieve the objective, establish or maintain identity and above all the products. For means can also disqualify their ends and question the identity of what or who uses them.

Therefore, it is not compatible with the desired image of an ecologically oriented firm as "ecological" if the firm simultaneously produces products that either have harmful side-effects themselves or whose manufacture results in the production of poisons which are disposed of improperly. In the same way, it is often a problem leading to paradox for trade union-owned enterprises to preserve their identity as representatives of the workers and simultaneously be committed to management objectives which lead or entice them to employ profit-oriented enterprise and personnel policies.

In working out a strategy, it is of utmost importance to assess the risks of failure first, which are primarily given by making these self-negating feed-back structures (creating paradox). In this, both the external market, the potential consumers, and the internal market, the employees – their specific attribution of meaning and evaluation – need to be taken into consideration as communication partners.

Quite generally, the following circular schema can be established for planning processes:

1. Definitions of the enterprise's identity;
2. Definitions of the enterprise's objectives;
3. Definitions of the products (possibly divided into different product groups, i. e. business fields);
4. Definitions of the necessary organisational structures (possibly divided into different business sectors analogous to the business fields);

5. Definitions of strategies (for various sectors);
6. Definitions of operative measures, i. e. necessary activities;
7. Definitions of the characteristics with which the achievement of objectives or the occurrence of risks, i. e. approaching the limits of survival, are controlled;

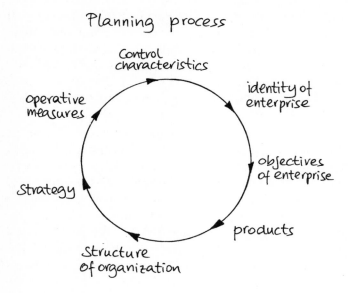

Fig. 13

Each of these points can be used as an approach to the planning process.

The circle can be closed by establishing the relationship to survival limits – as at the beginning. What obstacles can lead to the failure of a certain strategy? What ought one do or refrain from doing to render all planning efforts unsuccessful?

THE LIFE CYCLE OF PRODUCTS

Time may well be a great healer, but the ravages of time gnaw constantly, so that even the insight "only time will tell" is no consolation. The dimension of time is indispensable for all planning intentions. Life means change; nothing stays the way it is unless someone or something makes sure of it. And nothing evolves unless someone or something makes sure it does. We must also plan for "death". Ways of thinking, values and patterns of behaviour can soon become a thing of the past, and with them, customers' demands and the products that satisfy them also become a thing of the past.

In the human organism, all body cells (with the exception of the nerve cells) renew themselves within seven years at least once. Only this constant change enables living systems to remain the same. What does this mean for an enterprise and the life cycle of its products? Is there anything like a life after death for them? When a product dies out, which product inherits its buyers? In what rhythms should an optimal alternation of generations occur?

Computers are developing with breath-taking speed, Japanese firms have set new standards for ever faster model changes in the automobile industry. In the high-tech sector, the period between a product's birth and death is becoming shorter and shorter. In other areas, though, other dimensions of time can be reckoned with: The development of new "in" kinds of bread by no means threatens the market for traditional country-style bread, poppy-seed bread rolls or croissants etc.

Logically, the relationship between enterprise and consumers can only be preserved if supply and demand remain balanced. This may well be guaranteed on a long term basis as far as bread and other basic food stuffs are concerned, since the physical constitution of the consumers ensures a growing demand. A new generation of consumers ensures continuity of the market for babies' cots, baby clothes and literature for younger readers. In both cases, conditions are given that ensure a long life cycle for products. Enid Blyton's books, "Tom Sawyer" and "Pipi Longstocking" as long-term sellers can be found on the shelves in bookshops over decades (not to speak of the colossal bestseller for which royalties do not even have to be paid: the Bible). Where the markets are saturated, i. e. the customers' needs satisfied, change must take place on the side of the producer (e. g. by marketing new products) in order to keep the relationship in a constant range.

The central task of planning is to meet the extreme ups and downs of the cycles. Successful enterprises thus plan new products during the growth phase of the "old" ones and so do not fall into the trap of letting themselves be enticed to inactivity by deceptive profits during the saturation phase. These profits are usually highest in the saturation phase, but then it is often relatively late to start developing a new product.

It is essential to see the whole enterprise or the respective business unit, and not the single product, as unit of survival.

MONOPOLY VERSUS OPTIMAL MARKET SHARES

One of the sometimes clandestine, sometimes open objectives of managers seems to be to achieve a dominant market position with their products, brands, enterprises. From the view of radical market economy the question is what this makes possible or hinders according to a long-term cost-benefit-analysis of the monopoly.

Let us begin with a thought experiment. What would the consequences of this objective, monopoly status, be? It would mean a position of power in relationship to potential buyers. The buyer would be dependent on the monopolist as the only supplier, would have to buy whatever he supplied, without consideration of quality or price. For the enterprise, this lack of competition means it need not adapt its inner structures and processes to changes in the market. It can manufacture products whose life cycle lasts for ever. Trabant forever[7]. The products need never change. This only succeeds if the enterprise can reckon on an unchanging external environment.

In principle this would not be a problem if it worked this way. In the inaccessible bush in the Philippines you sometimes find native tribes whose structure and organisation have remained the same over centuries because the world they live in, or rather its conditions, have not changed. Cut off from the rest of the world, a stable balance between system and environment has established itself in which both are perfectly adapted to each other and do not need to develop.

The price for a monopolistic idyll is, in a certain sense, always a development standstill. Where no competition disturbs and threatens survival, adaptation to market conditions is guaranteed even for antiquated products.

7 Translator's note: The "Trabant" used to be the only automobile model in Eastern Germany.

However, the danger of rigidity due to one's own market power is limited in so far as it is linked to the isolation of the market. Competition can only be prevented where you can keep the borders closed to new products or even simply to information about them. It is thus advisable – even if it sounds paradoxical – to love your competitors so that they prevent you from missing your own development.

There are a number of other reasons to love your competitors as "fellow applicants". They are involved in the process of communication between buyers and sellers, in the question and answer game, the to and fro of mutual suggestion and enticement. And it is well-known that a hamburger stall somewhere all on its own has less turnover than each of three hamburger stalls all in the same place. It is thus necessary to utilise the synergetic potential provided by one's competitors.

The planning manager's ability to adapt must be high if he wants to cope with his task, namely adapting the enterprise to a complex market process. He has to manage turmoil and contradiction, form networks, see even hidden functional correlations. In this it is helpful to overcome all too simplifying black and white schemas in his analysis creatively by permanently assuming the outer perspective.

In the past, there were standards for measuring experience and empirically substantiated formulas for predicting the supposed future. The well-known curve of a product's life cycle represents the predicted and probable future of a product. Studies on clearly delineated segments of buyers who, particularly in the consumer goods area, seemed to make sociologically precise distinctions – but do so in almost no case today – are another example of such instruments. Today, on the other hand, there is no definitive measure for the required adaptability – either the manager's or the enterprise's.

The only relatively reliable standard for the quality of planning is probably the probability of the enterprise's survival in its environment. However, every plan must also take into consideration what cannot be planned. That means it must be vague enough, general, rough and simple enough it its definition of objectives, strategies and operative measures. Only thus is it possible to leave scope for what is not foreseeable and predictable, i. e. to avert risks and utilise options. Evolutionary planning must create the conditions for improvisation.

HIKING IN THE MOUNTAINS –
BETWEEN PLANNING AND IMPROVISATION

At this point, a story, can clarify better than any theories how strategy and improvisation, drifting and steering lead to achieving an objective, even if – or better: because – it was not originally set down precisely.

It is a description of a family's hike in the mountains, i. e. an organisation manifesting certain hierarchical structures with differing responsibilities, abilities and experiences of its members. The top manager (father of the family) reports:

1. Initial situation:

"The *Wilde Freyger* is a mountain in the Stubai Alps in Austria, altitude 3,418 m. Due to its altitude and position, the peak with its glaciers is more or less always conspicuously present as a challenge to all hikers in the Stubai Alps, as it was on the occasion of a several-day hike from hostel to hostel with my wife, my 13-year-old son and his friend of the same age.

Sometime during the morning, on our way from the 'Sulzenauer' to the 'Nürnberger' hostel, we began to discuss whether it might be possible to climb the *Wilde Freyger* together, although this was not included in our programme. As a relatively experienced mountaineer, I first tried to dismiss this idea as a fantasy. After all, there was a glacier to get across up there. We were by no means equipped for that, and besides, the two thirteen-year-olds had never been in these high alpine regions before.

But somehow it would be a fantastic thing if we succeeded! The closer we got to the 'Nürnberger' hostel, which would be a good starting point for an expedition to the *Freyger*, the more this idea became fixed in our heads, in mine, too."

2. Clarification of context

"An exact study of maps and route descriptions corroborated my fears. The *Freyger* glacier may well be relatively harmless, but only relatively so. There were, of course, one or two crevasses to cross. And depending on the weather, crossing a glacier is risky without crampons, ice picks and a short rope to secure yourself while crossing crevasses. Accordingly, one has to advise inexperienced mountain climbers against carrying out such plans.

A conversation with the manager of the hostel corroborated this assessment. However, if the conditions and the weather were particularly good, it would be quite possible to cross the glacier leading to a successful climb without any problems, even without specific equipment, but only if the conditions were particularly good ...

Other guests in the hostel report that such conditions might prevail the next day ... The manager of the hostel does not agree ..."

3. Planning:

"After careful consideration of all pros and cons and with a heavy heart we decided for reasons of safety only to climb the *Gamsspitze* (altitude 3,050 m) on the way to the *Freyger* and below the glacier region. As far as my level of expectation was concerned, I prepared myself for this emotionally. If more should come of it, which was not to be expected, all the better. We shall see ... But I really succeeded in adapting my expectations so that reaching the *Gamsspitze* with the two boys would be a completely satisfactory aim for me, too."

4. Action:

"Still early in the day, we reached the *Gamsspitze* after a quite exhausting climb – the boys walked along, sweating but cheerful, without whining or complaining.

While we sat and had a snack, I looked more and more longingly at the *Freyger* in front of us, almost close enough to touch. My wife and children probably felt the same. Directly below us was one of the first bigger patches of snow, a little bit above we could see the beginning of the glacier. The weather was really beautiful. It was possible that these were the particularly good conditions discussed yesterday evening.

We decided to climb on in the direction of the *Freyger* for as long as we all felt that we were not taking any serious risks. Should there appear to be any risk, we would turn back.

With this holy oath we started off again. This decision had given us all enough security. The first patch of snow was no problem, tremendous corn snow with a good grip, an absolute pleasure.

Suddenly we were at the foot of the glacier. Now it was becoming serious, demanding a new decision. We watched a group of mountain climbers climbing down over the glacier in our direction. When they reached us, they told us that ideal conditions indeed prevailed: gripping firn right to the top, absolutely no problem even without crampons. However, there was one open crevasse that could not be bypassed. In order to cross this obstruction without risk, you really needed an ice pick and ropes for safety.

As we didn't have these things, we decided to climb up to this crevasse and then turn back. Even that would make a nice glacier walk. A first experience for our kids and not an everyday one for my wife and me. We parents were satisfied, and so were the children. We started walking; it was quite exhausting, but not dangerous, the weather stayed clear and beautiful.

After a while, a mountaineer overtook us who, strangely enough, had a scarf hanging over his eyes. While I stepped aside to let him pass, my wife started talking to him. I waited, mumbling to myself about this unnecessary interruption. It was an Englishman who had forgotten his sunglasses: quite a problem at 3,200 m on a glacier in the brilliant July sunshine.

This Englishman was a funny character: He had an ice pick, rope, clampons, everything good and expensive, but no sunglasses. My wife remembered that she had an extra old pair of sunglasses in her backpack. She gave them to him. Then, before he went on his way, the subject turned to the crevasse we could already see above us. He could secure us with his equipment, couldn't he ... he offered. After a moment of hesitation I was prepared to give it a try, even with the boys. Their eyes were shining. Not a trace of fear. OK, we'll have a go!

Great adventure: When we reached the crevasse the whole crew, expertly secured, jumped across it one after the other. What a treat! After half an hour we reached the summit without danger, sweating and happy – the boys because they'd made it, we adults because we managed it without endangering our kids, although we had neither planned nor prepared for it. At home this would have seemed absolutely unjustifiably dangerous. We were all proud of ourselves, our energy and our cleverness.

After a proper break and a fantastic view all around we climbed back down. The Englishman accompanied us to the crevasse, the same procedure as before. We said goodbye, he moved off, and we followed him, a little slower.

That evening in the hostel we told the new arrivals about the *Freyger* and our ascent, the boys were celebrated, they deserved it. That day we achieved something absolutely unexpected and unplanned."

From the view of evolutionary planning, the analysis of this success story of a (mountain) peak performance shows the following correlations and prerequisites:

As the ones with experience, the adults were able to orient themselves toward the children's assumed upper limits when establishing mutual goals. The children, who were less experienced, were able to accept this evaluation of their possibilities.

Together each was able to communicate the certainty to the others that if new information arose, the definition of the goal could be discussed anew and revised at any time. The new data was examined for its information content and used to reassess the situation.

In the same way it was possible to conclude an exchange of commodities on the way to supplement their resources at the right time to ensure success.

Above all, though, both the experienced mountaineers and the less experienced were able to utilise arising uncertainties in such a way that new options resulted that used the arising uncertainties in such a way that new options resulted that used the arising uncertainties in such a way that new options resulted that used the arising uncertainties in such a way …

Recipes

- *Observe observers observing (others and themselves)! What do they focus their attention on? How do they find their orientation? What standards of evaluation do they use to explain their willingness to give their trust (money) to the enterprise or the product they are observing?*
- *Don't only plan for the survival of your enterprise, your business unit, your product, but also for the survival of the respective market.*
- *Accept contradiction, ambivalence and conflict as inevitable. They do not disappear if you ignore them. On the contrary.*

- *Utilise the positive force of "negative" thinking: Plan failure carefully and systematically! In this way you find out quickest what you ought better refrain from doing.*
- *Ensure the inclusion of the important environments in the planning process. Someone within the enterprise, division etc. should represent the views and interests of these environments. This clarifies scope of action and its limits. Employ "troublemakers" for the planning process.*
- *Focus not only on what has to be done, but also on what must be refrained from. It is advisable to make cost-benefit calculations for both.*
- *Utilise uncertainties as a chance to open up new options, plan for improvisation!*

7. Culture

> "Believing, with Max Weber, that man is an animal
> suspended in webs of significance he himself has spun,
> I take culture to be those webs."
> Clifford Geertz[1]

> "Behaviour must be paid attention to ..."
> Clifford Geertz[2]

DANGEROUS AND OTHER PATTERNS

The concept "corporate culture" is surprisingly popular. And as with many other magic formulas top executives have to grapple with, the wishy-washy answer to the question "How do you do that?" shows that we are once again dealing with one of those nebulous, unlovable abstractions.

If we take a look at how the cultural experts – ethnologists and anthropologists – use this concept, we note that we have been occupying ourselves with cultural questions all the time. The scientific meaning of culture has little to do with premières in municipal theatres, opening days of exhibitions by the society for the promotion of fine arts or poetry readings, but rather with organisation and semantic import. Culture can be understood as "interlocking systems of interpretable symbols" which "provide a frame of interpretation for social events, behaviours, institutions and processes".[3]

---

1 C. Geertz (1973): Thick Description ... In: The Interpretation of Cultures. Selected Essays. New York (Basic Books).
2 ib.
3 ib.

If for us "organisation" means ordered patterns of behaviour, culture forms the more inclusive system in which these patterns of behaviour are connected with some kind of construction of reality (meanings). Both areas of phenomena, menu/recipe and eating/cooking are inseparably linked, patterns of interaction produce and stabilise patterns of semantic import, patterns of semantic import produce and confirm patterns of interaction. Culture is a product and a means of communication.

You are sitting in a restaurant and have an unspeakable mush on your plate. You look in the menu and read "Mousse aux ...", and immediately you have a scheme of interpretation at your disposal that gives rise to countless ideas on what ingredients have been used, how the chef achieved the wonderful consistency of his mush, what the whole thing might possibly taste like, that you might react to it with an itchy rash and ought better send it back, but then the tail-coated waiter would look at you indignantly ..., all this together is culture.

Objectively, it is quite appropriate to see enterprises as South Sea Islanders or Indian tribes. These practice certain belief systems, taboos and rituals which unite the participants in one world view allowing joint organised action. The larger an enterprise and the more different people with different practical tasks it includes, the more sophisticated the entire cultural system composed of several subcultures will be. There is the subculture of the auditing division, whose values and interpretations have little similarity to those of the research and development division. Yet all these subcultures can only live and/or survive as elements of a superior organisational structure to which the respective other subculture, for which the world is constructed in a completely different way, also belongs.

What, then, is the effect of culture?

- It offers distinctive categories for perception (What must we look out for?).
- It offers a frame of interpretation for signs and symbols (What means what?).
- It limits the behavioural possibilities (What is forbidden?).
- It increases the probability of certain behaviours (What is stipulated?).

– It defines the market and the market values for behaviour (What do you get for what?).

On several layers, culture thus provides the basis for individual and mutual orientation and assessment of actions. To give an illustration: In the same way as we can distinguish several structural levels of a water lily above and below the water surface, the permanence and durability of which vary considerably, it appears quite useful for business transactions to describe levels of varying longevity for culture, too.

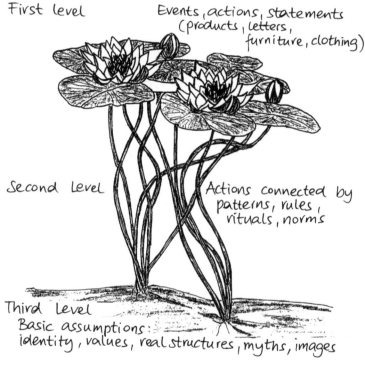

First level — Events, actions, statements (products, letters, furniture, clothing)

Second level — Actions connected by patterns, rules, rituals, norms

Third level — Basic assumptions: identity, values, real structures, myths, images

Fig. 14

Level 1

Behaviour: This part of culture, comparable with the blossoms of the water lily on the surface of the water, can be observed directly. If, as

133

a manager, you realise that your behaviour is not helping you to achieve your goals, you can initiate change on this level by changing your behaviour.

Level 2

Patterns: Under water, water lilies are connected with each other and form patterns and rules. Similarly the behaviour of an enterprise's employees is connected (= organisation). There are ritualised processes, either purposefully planned and controlled as in most areas of production, or ones that develop over time, such as conference rituals. Such rules and patterns are always maintained by several persons. Changes in the behaviour of an individual might interfere with them, but cannot be the sole reason for purposeful change in a certain direction.

Level 3

Basic assumptions: Comparable with the water lily's roots and probably most difficult to change, the belief systems and reality constructions of the persons maintaining a culture form the foundation for the mutually realised rules and patterns as well as for individual behaviour.

However, this comparison between culture and the water lily does have one serious drawback: It suggests a linear cause-and-effect relationship between roots, patterns and blossoms. But, contrary to water lily blossoms, changed behaviour can indeed join together to make new patterns and rules. And if there are a lot of changes on the behavioural level, many basic assumptions on reality are no longer confirmed, so that finally they change, too. In a culture, the wheel turns full circle: the blossoms can also change the roots (although the reverse is more likely, of course, and therefore occurs more frequently).

As your own culture is (has become) self-evident, you only actually realise what the culture of your own enterprise or division is like in comparison with others. Newcomers and/or novices notice it, though. They rapidly sense or hear what is and what is not mandatory in this enterprise or this division. The culture of an enterprise is therefore always what is invisible, too, the only seemingly soft reality, which is a hard nut to crack for the ostensibly so hard reality of business administration and strict management directives ...

The focal point of our analysis of corporate cultures is concentrated on where cultural patterns can determine the success and failure of an enterprise as well as that of its individual employees. In accordance with the principle of the positive force of "negative" thinking propagated above, the pathological patterns shall be emphasised here, i. e. patterns which in our experience increase the probability of failure sooner or later. Or to put it differently: Nobody can say what is possible, i. e. which forms of corporate culture are or might be compatible with survival, but one can definitely establish what is not possible, or what is only possible at a high economic price for the enterprise or high individual price (physical or psychological) for its employees.

It is just the same in medicine. You can give someone very precise instructions on how he is most likely to ruin his liver thoroughly, quickly and inexpensively. However, you cannot tell anyone how to give his liver a treat at Christmas or how to do it any other kind of favour.

If you want to influence the culture of an enterprise, refraining from whatever is likely to be harmful and dangerous is one of the guidelines you can use for orientation. There is no optimal, healthy, standard corporate culture, but there are dysfunctional patterns which are even more likely to produce problems (though even then it is not certain!).

The typology of such "dangerous" cultural patterns presented here has the same drawbacks as all typologies. It attempts to describe the common interests distilled out of many individual cases. The results depend not only on what is really happening, but also on what distinctions the observer makes, what choices he makes, what he regards as important or unimportant etc. The observer always idealises and schematises, which means that distinctions and particulars are always lost. On the other hand, however, common interests, family resemblances become visible which would not have been noticed without these simplifications. Thus "real" corporate cultures or organisations are only as similar as the ideal types described here, sometimes related more to the one, sometimes more to the other.[4]

THE ORGANISATION OF BALANCE

In order to survive, living systems have to balance opposing tendencies and organise contradictions. They maintain their identity by changing and find stability in motion – like a cyclist who can only keep his balance when he has reached a certain speed, or a tightrope walker who has to swing to the right and left to keep her balance. They require both ordering activities and processes dissolving this order, both constancy and change, both housewifery, violations of rules and creativity.

Thus the question of how change and balance between order and chaos is structured in an organisation within the dimension of time – on the level of actions as well as ideas – forms our guideline for describing corporate cultures. However, we by no means equate the principles of order and chaos used here with a good and bad bipolarity. In the last analysis, the distinction between order and chaos relevant for organisations refers only to the predictability or nonpredictability of the behaviour of living systems.

Since organisations are composed of behaviour, we observe what function (effect) it can have within the framework of balancing processes. To this end it would be sensible to coordinate behaviour purposefully. If we consider chaos and order as contradictory results of human action, the effect of what we do and don't do, our actions and omissions, can be distinguished according to four types:

1. You actively create order within the organisation, thereby counteracting the development of chaos and refraining from everything that disintegrates order.
2. You actively create chaos, thereby disintegrating order and refraining from everything that counteracts chaos.
3. You refrain from everything that might promote or reduce order or chaos, i. e. you have no active effect on chaos or order.

4 Max Weber introduced the concept of the "ideal type" in sociology; c. f. M. Weber (1913): Über einige Kategorien der verstehenden Soziologie. In: Gesammelte Aufsätze zur Wissenschaftslehre. Tübingen (Mohr).

4. You actively create order and you actively create chaos. You have an actively promoting effect towards the two contradictory goals, i. e. you are ambivalent and equivocal towards chaos and order.

Preferences for one of these four types of action (level 1) characterise the culture of a division, or rather certain assumptions and theories (level 3) about the world lead to certain culturally promoted actions. Most of the time, however, actions of the four different types are combined to form patterns (level 2) which enable each individual actor to use his own abilities more in this or that direction, and yet still ensure a balance between the contradictory tendencies on the level of culture as a whole.

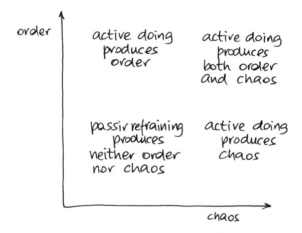

Fig. 15

The rank of the four types of action presented here is different for diverse organisations with their manifold tasks and goals. Wherever developmental processes, i. e. change, are necessary for survival, the behaviour of the artist gains particular importance (top right in the diagram), as it stands for creativity: the disintegration of order and creation of order. This ambivalent function may well be split up between different persons and groups within the framework of division of labour, but it is important that both sides realise a balance towards both tendencies. If one side asserts itself in the sense of gaining a subculture, the entire system starts to totter.

137

Corporate cultures concentrate the attention of the employees on certain meanings and assess them positively or negatively. This renders culture a decisive factor which controls a firm's internal exchange market for behaviour. It determines selection among the employees. Anyone who works in a firm has to assert himself on a particular market, i. e. he must do or refrain from doing what is highly rated. Anyone who cannot do this will soon leave again or be dismissed. The personal exchange system and the behaviour of each employee has to fit the cultural patterns of the enterprise.

Let us give an example: Recently, a reputable banking establishment started an elaborate academic trainee program for professionals. In its course, particularly highly qualified young university graduates were kept away from regular routine tasks for approximately one and a half years after joining the enterprise. Instead they were allowed to snoop around in all areas without any pressure, get to know them, get a clear idea of them, develop their own views etc. In certain intervals, the training division organised meetings in which the young people were to exchange their experiences, ideas and interests under the supervision of tutors. At these meetings, the next stages and goals of the personal scouting tour through the enterprise were then arranged in accordance with the individual qualification focus. Modelled on sourdough, an explicit goal of this costly plan was to generate a pool of young, unconventional, lateral thinkers and dissenters who, once they had taken over regular functions, could then change the enterprise's "rigid" organisational culture.

To the surprise of the appointed tutors, it was established that the young lateral thinkers started ascertaining and adopting the rules for survival in the enterprise like lightning. Within a few months, the cleverest of the young people were excellently informed on who has a lot or little to say in the enterprise, where and how and by whom decisions are made, who is important for one's own career, what behaviour might be beneficial or detrimental to one's own career, who in the firm has a good or bad relationship with whom, what role the staff council has etc. In short, within six months the young "sourdough guys" were behaving like old-established pros in the existing corporate culture.

Presumably the internal balance sheet of the trainees in reference to the two variations a) officially expected sourdough behaviour versus b) using the existing rules in accordance with one's own de-velopmental interests, showed on average higher gains for varia-tion b). To the disappointment of the training programme's initia-tors, the personal behaviour of the young, highly qualified employ-ees followed the beaten track of the existing corporate culture.

THE MADLY CHAOTIC AND THE PSYCHOSOMATICALLY ORDERED PATTERN

To demonstrate, let us turn to two of the above-mentioned "danger-ous" cultural patterns.

On the chaotic side of the spectrum, we find the madly chaotic pattern of corporate culture. It is remarkable because, in the long run, it is not so very easy to prevent order developing – all on its own – through processes of self-organisation. The maintenance of chaotic non-structures (i. e. preventing the development of struc-tures) must thus be considered an achievement, i. e. something that is accomplished actively by doing or not doing. Let us see how this can best be accomplished:

Reality construction in these enterprises is extremely soft, i. e. there is no consensus on how to describe reality. What was regarded as "true" yesterday can be considered "false" today and "true" again tomorrow. To a large extent, communication is characterised by am-biguity, contradiction, vagueness and paradox. The respective mes-sages are disqualified so that nobody can be even vaguely certain what the other person means. Behaviour with a high market value yesterday might suddenly be completely devalued today and be in great demand again tomorrow. The arbitrariness of rules and values is accompanied by the softness of this reality construction. The rule seems to be that there are no rules. If you regard these rules under the aspect of their constancy and reliability on the one hand, and their changeability and adaptability on the other, the paradox seems to apply that these enterprises cannot change their rules because they themselves change too quickly.

As far as reality construction is concerned, everyone in this cul-ture seems to pursue an either/or pattern, so that conflicts ensue over who is actually "right". Everyone tries to get his own private currency generally established. There seems to be no possibility of several views existing legitimately and appropriately side by side.

139

Contradictory views stand side by side simultaneously and disqualify each other.

No distinct roles and coalitions can be identified, and relationship definitions change constantly. For this reason no one manages to attain a clear picture of them. This applies for the consultant observing from the outside as well as for the employees seeking a firm and reliable relationship definition. Nobody knows whether relationships are hierarchical or equal. The organigram is only paper, although – suddenly and unexpectedly – role requirements are (may be) demanded which are (may be) forgotten again just as suddenly. No one is certain about the kind of relationship he has to the others. Friendliness and distant reservation are offered in unpredictable succession. This lack of clarity also applies to role definitions and job descriptions. There are no clear contracts and no agreement is reached on who should do what and who is responsible for what.

There are no binding norms, either on an individual or on a collective level, telling us what emotional reactions are appropriate to which behaviour. It does not seem possible to come to an agreement on whether a certain behaviour should be classified as "strong", "active" and "bad" for instance, or as "weak", "passive" and "good". The same applies to the assessment of the individuals manifesting these modes of behaviour. In particular, this has an effect on the uncertainty as to who wins the laurels for which successes and bears the blame for which failures.

The result is often general confusion. Nobody knows who does what for what motives and in accordance with which cost-benefit analyses. Everyone feels exposed to all conceivable alternating feelings. This results in conflicts boiling over from time to time, although there seem to be no comprehensible explicit triggers for it (or at most trifling reasons). However, some kind of pseudo harmony seemingly lacking any objective justification may also prevail.

The cultural patterns presented here were first described in families in which one member turned mad. Whether madness is regarded as "cause" or "effect" in this case has no relevance to our subject of investigation. The result is continuously changing rules and a high degree of emotional and intellectual confusion in all concerned. Something similar happens in enterprises, although usually without madness developing.

A bewildering style of communication develops as soon as subjects are addressed which entail the danger of one or another of the employees being officially blamed or becoming the official winner in the rat race. This gives the participants the feeling that the firm ground of reality is falling from beneath their feet, as if they were standing on quicksand, without knowing what is actually real and what is not, or what is actually being said. There is no consensus on the meaning of the participants' behaviour. This generally triggers individual tensions. One feels urged to search for a hidden meaning, the thread of the conversation and a focus for one's attention. This is the ground on which rumours, conspiratorial theories and paranoid fears grow.

Someone who goes into such a firm as a newcomer often feels tempted to counteract the confusing methods of communication and seemingly chaotic interaction. He feels obliged to ensure clarity, unambiguity and ordered, recognisable rules. In his effort to establish lucidity, he starts organising and tries to exert control over the others in a direct or indirect fashion. He becomes the "advocate" of a harder reality construction and feels responsible for establishing binding rules and external structures. He often sees his task in ensuring that conflicts are detected and ultimately resolved. But the more he attempts to assume this clarifying function, the more ambiguous the style of communication generally becomes.

All this may urge him, just like all the other interactants, to participate in the game of debasing each other and the firm itself. Accordingly, fluctuation of employees in enterprises or divisions with this kind of culture is very high: Anyone who can, escapes from loss of orientation and (self-) debasement. This is a bad market for his products. The only ones who stay are employees for whom this lack of clarity is combined with the promise of great personal advantage in the future (whatever that may be).

The counterpole and contrast to this madly chaotic pattern is the psychosomatically ordered pattern. It was first described in families in which serious psychosomatic disturbances occurred. This cultural pattern seems to be connected with the heightened risk of physical illness. It would no doubt be worthwhile to study systematically the extent to which such forms of corporate culture correlate with increased sick-leave amongst the employees.

Reality construction in these enterprises is extremely hard, i. e. there is a clear consensus on how reality is to be described, and this is not open to discussion. Whatever was regarded as "true" yesterday, has to be considered "true" tomorrow and for ever after. Social rules are treated as unchangeable, like laws of nature. All interactants seem to assume that messages always have a clear and unambiguous meaning. Everyone thinks he is absolutely sure what the other means or does not mean. The hardness of this reality construction is accompanied by the rigidity and unchangeability of the rules of interaction. What applied once, always applies. If you then look at these rules under the aspect of their continuity on the one hand and their adaptability on the other, you realise that they cannot change (or only with difficulty) and react to new environmental requirements.

In this culture, too, everyone seems to submit to an either/or pattern in his construction of reality. Nevertheless, there is no argument about who is right, since all have to share the same beliefs and unwavering goals. As a hard definition of reality exists, there is no space for conflict about the truth of statements. Here, too, there is no possibility of several points of view being justified and applicable simultaneously. Viewed from an inner perspective, there are no opposing tendencies. In a very narrow-minded way, only one side of opposing tendencies is ever cultivated fully.

Opposing points of view can never be set out openly, side by side, at the same time, because anyone who does not share the cultural values is excluded, i. e. he will be fired. He does not find a market. Therefore open conflicts are tabu, they are avoided like the plague, negative feelings may not and cannot be expressed openly, only mutual appreciation. Deviation is frightening.

Formally, there are clear roles and subsystems, but they are often denied ("We are all one big family"). Consequently, there is a certain amount of doubt about the quality of relationships and coalitions, although this confusion, contrary to the madly chaotic pattern, is not established actively but produced by refraining from something. One person quite naturally expects the other to obey the obvious rules, without this having to be pointed out specifically. Normality and the mutual satisfaction of natural, normative, pre-conceived expectations is highly rated.

Individually and collectively, it is obvious what emotional reaction is appropriate to what behaviour. These standards define whether a mode of behaviour should be classified as "strong", "active" and "bad" or as "weak", "passive" and "good". The same applies to the assessment of the individuals manifesting these modes of behaviour. Individuals are readily prepared to accept responsibility, but just as readily develop guilty feelings, the fear of making mistakes and being caught in the process. Officially, taking over responsibility entails the danger of being blamed and is thus avoided if possible. On the other hand, everyone seems to wander around secretly with a vacuum cleaner that sucks up responsibility and seems unable to limit his own sphere. Thus, uncertainty prevails as to who really bears the responsibility for what.

The feelings associated with this cause problems for those involved, primarily because they always expect themselves to have the "right" feelings or no (inappropriate) feelings at all. Whenever they get into conflict, they have to sweep one side of their ambivalence out of the way, since it is not on demand in this cultural form. This may be one of the reasons for health risks. The organisation of physical processes does not comply with a world view free of contradiction.

Communication dies as soon as any subjects are mentioned which entail the danger of allocating blame to one or another of the employees. This triggers a feeling of helplessness and paralysis in the participants, a feeling of not being able to do anything, and results in physical problems (headache, migraine etc.).

Anyone who enters such a firm or institution as a newcomer often feels called upon to work as an antidepressant or nurse. However, in doing so he merely confirms the rule that conflict must be avoided.

He or she soon develops a sense of failure, the impression of not fulfilling the task, of having to do everything better. This self-derogation is set against the demand of revaluing the others. Fluctuation of employees is only minor, mutual bonds and loyalties are very high. The common good has precedence over self-interest. Personal gain lies in the fact that one can credit one's own account with a considerable amount of fellow feeling, reliability and adherence to all the unchangeable and eternal norms.

The two patterns described here are, of course, extreme examples that are rarely found to this perfection. The extreme psychosomatic-ordered culture, which also includes a strong totalitarian moral demand for fellow feeling, is hardly to be found in private enterprises. It is more likely to occur in ecclesiastical or social institutions in which selection of employees and their inner currencies ensures that supply and demand are preserved in this market.

However, the aspect of hard reality, the demand for strict rationality and the disqualification of inappropriate emotions, the tabu on resolving certain conflicts openly, fear of failure and threats of separation are widespread in private enterprises, too. Managers do not choose migraines and headaches as symptoms as frequently as heart attacks and stomach ulcers, but to a great extent, psychosomatic factors can be made responsible for their origin as well.

The mad chaotic pattern is more likely to be found in artistic and – contrary to expectation – scientific spheres in which each individual tries to attain his right to autonomy and fears that his creativity will die if rules are established. Thus from the outside a permanent struggle for power can be observed which is experienced on the inside as the struggle to safeguard one's own freedom. We know of several public scientific institutes in which (seen from the outside) seemingly infinitely labourious voting and decision-making procedures are in practice. This guarantees that all employees have the impression that nothing of consequence is done without their assistance. Of course, it is not always possible to develop an effective organisation in this way, especially as these labourious decisions are often not taken down in the minutes and thus forgotten again. In quite a similar way and for similar reasons artist cooperatives usually fail economically, too.

Both cultural patterns are probably "dangerous" because they limit the possible options of the employees too much and either do not permit ambivalence and contradiction where they might be useful (for the purpose of postponing decisions and actions) or cannot resolve them where freedom of ambivalence and contradiction might be necessary (in order to make decisions and act).

This kind of pattern, however, always presents a market for potential employees whose personality and values can develop here.

In short: Every enterprise gets the employees it deserves, i. e. the employees suiting its culture.

ESTABLISHING CULTURE

Although culture has been interpreted very generally at the beginning of this chapter as "interlocking systems of interpretable symbols" which provide a "frame of interpretation for social events, behaviours, institutions and processes", this can be formulated somewhat more precisely with regard to the sphere of activity of managers. Corporate culture can be regarded as a system of behavioural standards, values and basic assumptions which as such provides the foundations for individual orientation and assessment of activities in an enterprise.

So far we have treated this subject from the outer perspective of analytical diagnostics. The practicing executive asks himself how he can influence and change what he sees and finds impractical.

The answer to this question is as simple as it is succinct. Managers establish the culture of their organisational sphere of influence through all the things they do or refrain from doing day by day. It is of no consequence whether this formation of culture by everyday actions occurs consciously or unconsciously.

Edgar Schein[5] has examined how managers with a reputation for establishing the culture of an enterprise permanently within a short period of time actually do this. The result: Consciously or unconsciously, managers express their convictions by taking note of and rewarding certain modes of behaviour, by forming roles and by reacting to critical incidents in a certain way. They also apply their specific standards of values when recruiting, selecting, promoting and dismissing personnel. The employees perceive all this in order to construct a frame of orientation for themselves which allows them, in turn, to survive and develop within the sphere of influence of a supervisor.

These highly effective mechanisms to firmly establish a manager's convictions in the daily life of an organisation are supported

---

5   E. H. Schein (1985): Organisational Culture and Leadership. A Dynamic View. San Francisco (Jessey-Bass).

or confused by messages embodied in the structure of the organisation, its routine functions, its anecdotes and legends and finally
even in its formal models. The culture of an enterprise is, so to speak,
the sediment of the behavioural standards, values and basic assumptions depicted by successful executives in their everyday activities.
From the perspective of radical market economy, a manager's values, his internal currency and his accounting methods determine the
most important terms of trade for in-house commodity exchange.
Not all modes of behaviour fetch the same price.

Since only something that attracts attention becomes a commodity, it is not surprising that Edgar Schein also comes to the conclusion
that a manager passes on central formative cultural messages to his
employees through what he takes note of, measures and controls.

There are, for instance, executives who want to know what costs
how much at any time, no matter how inconvenient. If, in addition,
these people are influential personalities, the standard "cheap is
good" begins to develop. In turn, employees then try to succeed in
reducing costs, their boss regards them highly, others try to emulate
them ... The evolving spiral of ever increasing cost orientation may
influence an entire generation of managers in an enterprise.

The second important variable in a manager's behaviour are his
reactions to critical incidents and crises in the organisation. It makes
a significant difference whether an executive elegantly side steps and
sacrifices one of his employees to appease the "Gods" when his sector gets into difficulties and provokes the "wrath of the Gods", or
whether he opens a large, protective umbrella under which all his
employees find shelter. Usually this executive then has to carry not
only the umbrella, but also everything that rains down on it.

Another possibility would be to accept criticism calmly with no
ifs ands or buts if it seems correct, and then devote oneself very
strictly to analysing and working out solutions to the problems. All
of these reactions are perceived and assessed very differently by the
employees.

All three situations have two factors in common: the attentive-
ness with which the employees observe the behaviour of their supervisor in this crisis, and the fact that through his behaviour he has
a specific formative influence on the cultural rules and patterns of
the division. Another reminder that as an executive you cannot not
lead.

The fact that formal statements on the philosophy of the enterprise, statutes, public confessions and appeals are to be found last on the list of formative cultural mechanisms is absolutely plausible from the perspective of radical market economy. Compared to the consistent behaviour manifested by an important supervisor, guidelines printed on glossy paper are merely low-value commodities, minor economic goods.

Here are two more exemplary stories taken straight from life:

In comparison with international companies, a German food industry enterprise was successful in its market niche because of its high quality standards and rigorously hygienic production. This rendered it possible to reduce wastage and guarantee the merchants a low probability of the products perishing. The prices achieved because of this resulted internally in no special attention being paid to costs. The appearance of competitors, however, necessitated rethinking. In order to support cost-consciousness, the manager set the cost structure of the sectors on the agenda of the weekly meeting of division chiefs as a fixed item.

In the meeting on Tuesday, 5 December, the lab chief reported that costs had been exceeded by nine percent in the month of November. He was well prepared (with transparency-sheets and flip charts) for the manager's expected question and would have been able to talk extensively on his concise "How did that happen?". But after approximately three minutes his explanations were interrupted with a just as concise but not unfriendly "OK", before he could even switch on the overhead projector.

On the same day, three hours later, the manager takes a walk through the works. On one production line he discovers that milk leaking from one of the pumps is forming a pool on the floor and has apparently been doing so for quite a while. His fit of rage over the "mess on the floor" amazes and disturbs the entire team.

The events of this day had a formative influence on culture. The results: costs are still being more or less ignored, cleaning is more important than ever, and cleanliness of the floor has priority over keeping an eye on critical machine parts.

An example for a successful alteration: In the process of re-organisation, the managing board of a company decided to delegate important decisions relating to work to decentralised team structures. As the team members were still unused to dealing with changed competence and responsibility structures, many problems were sent back to the original decision-making board (to be solved). This was accepted to start with in order to keep the business running, although it opposed the goal of reorganisation.

However, since top management was certain that the changed requirements needed team structures, they decided on two counter strategies. Top management consciously put up with the paradoxicalness of this and determined that the installed teams had to make decisions and must undergo team training to learn how. Secondly – consciously acknowledging the risk – they no longer reacted to problems sent back to them. Within two months, the new procedure was running smoothly.

We regard the perspectives of corporate cultures developed here as very useful for executives, because they follow a consistent "perpetrator model". This means executives are not cultural victims but cultural perpetrators. They are responsible not only for the quality of their formative influence on culture by what they do or refrain from doing, but also for its intensity. The more influence a manager attains in an enterprise, the more significant the meaning of the standards, values and reality constructions he communicates in his everyday behaviour on the company's in-house exchange markets.

Recipes

– *Observe your company through the eyes of an ethnologist. Do not take anything for granted and examine rites and customs. Which Gods are being worshipped? Which (exchange) values guide activities? How do you behave and dress? What language is spoken? When are what kind of emotions and thoughts manifested? How does one feel and think here? What do you have to do to become the victim of ritual sacrifice? Which myths serve to interpret everyday life? Which stories are told? etc.*

– *Observe the questions or surprise of new associates at the rules, myths and standards of value in your enterprise or division. You should even encourage them to raise these questions. In the process you will receive important information on elements of the orga-*

nisation's culture that you have probably been taking for granted for a long time.

— Contemplate whether you find a market for your behaviour in this culture with your way of thinking, feeling and speaking.

— If you want to influence the culture, you are playing with the balance between order and chaos. You should know, however, that processes of balance often follow a paradoxical logic. If you emphasise tendencies that question the given order in a very ordered system, this might give rise to counter regulations which lend more weight to the orderly side of the balance. Or vice versa.

8. Sex Roles

"Men and women simply don't fit together!"
Loriot[1]

"Act always as to increase the number of choices!"
Heinz von Foerster[2]

SMALL DIFFERENCES, BIG DIFFERENCES

Let's begin with a quiz. Here are four scenes and the question is: Who is X?

In each case, one of the following four answers is possible:

X is
a) a woman,
b) a man,
c) can be both,
d) do not know.

The scenes:

1) It's late again. X comes home from the office and changes. Then X sits down at the laid table, sighs with pleasure and is delighted about the pleasant smell coming from the kitchen. This is going to be a nice cosy evening, X thinks.
2) The (female) division chief and the boss of another division have invited X to a birthday party at the pub round the corner. X

---

1 Loriot (1983): Dramatische Werke. Zürich (Diogenes) p. 116.
2 H. von Foerster (1973): On Constructing a Reality. In: F. E. Preiser (Ed.): Environmental Design Research. Stroudsburg, PA (Dowden, Hutchinson & Ross), pp. 35–46.

had actually planned to get home earlier today. Undecided, X puts the invitation in the drawer of her/his desk. "Well, I'll just pop in for a quick one!"

3) Wednesday, 8.30 am. X is sitting on the settee and thinking about what has to be done today: shopping, cleaning windows, baking cakes for tomorrow's children's party, fetching daughter from kindergarten, taking her to her gym class, finishing some sewing, cooking for tonight ...

4) The telephone rings. "It's pretty busy today", X thinks and picks up the receiver. "A private call for you, your father", announces the secretary. "I'll only trouble you for a second as I know things are always pretty hectic in your office. But you know that it's Mother's birthday next week. Have you any idea what I could give her?"

5) At 10 o'clock sharp the project team for the introduction of new quality standards meets in the conference room. X is conducting today's meeting and explains the agenda.

It should not be too difficult to solve the riddle, so there are no flower prizes (not to mention washing machines!). It's as clear as daylight: The best example for housewifery is housewifery, the best example for men's work is a job. Typically female, typically male, all biologically pre-determined – or not?

In German, this can easily lead to linguistic confusion. Men are masculine, women are feminine – this can be seen immediately and at first sight. The small biological difference is equated with differences in behaviour, personality, abilities and inabilities. From the relatively hard reality of physical endowment (it is not impossible to change it, but would necessitate quite elaborate surgical skills) it is only too easy to conclude that an individual's behaviour patterns (production of behaviour depends on the market) are also biologically pre-determined and unchangeable.

In English, the danger of these seductive simplifications is not so great because there are two different terms, one for (biological) sex and one for (social) gender. Use of language makes it quite obvious that they are not the same and cannot be measured with the same yardstick.

From an early age, girls and boys have to supply different markets with their behaviour, so they cultivate different abilities from the very beginning, develop different modes of behaviour for the market and often different values, too. Like all processes of evolution, this is not one in which the environment can unequivocally determine what individual resources will be promoted and what patterns of behaviour selected; however, the varying focus of attention of the individuals surrounding a child or adolescent determines what becomes a tradable ware. Only something we are aware of becomes a ware.

This begins with the different tasks assigned to girls and boys at home, continues with the different games they play (girls more person-oriented: father-mother-child; boys more competitive: football), and finally leads to the promotion of different talents in school. The result is that men and women bring different abilities into their professional life.

As far as personnel managers are concerned, one of the strengths of female managers is the fact that they are interested in the well-being of the people they work with, are able to conduct difficult consultations with employees, and cooperate well and willingly instead of struggling along on their own. They also know how to incorporate emotional components as well as rational arguments in decisions. According to personnel managers, male executives tend to solve problems rationally, they favour hierarchic organisational structures, their behaviour is more competitive and they try to leave their emotions out of it. If they are not successful in this they do not usually regard it as a sign of warmth, but as a shortcoming ("I was too emotional today!").

Personnel managers' experiences with female and male executives not only tell us something about these two groups of people, of course, but also about personnel managers' patterns and forms of perception. People perceive selectively and to a certain extent always mutually confirm their respective prejudices. Nevertheless, the assessment given here cannot be denied; however, the last few years have shown that female executives are increasingly manifesting modes of behaviour described as "male" and obviously feel happy about it. There are also enough male executives who manifest person-oriented qualities attributed to women – without, however, being called "feminine" (whatever that may mean). This may well signify that both patterns of behaviour find their market within enterprises irrespective of who is offering them.

In general, however, quite specific expectations are linked with the behaviour of men and women and then become "attributes" ("Men are ..., women are ..."). They are regarded as mutually exclusive. The "feminine" elements and abilities of men and the "masculine" elements and abilities of women are thus not often perceived and/or solicited. Anyone whose behaviour is different to what is expected from them is in danger of being subjected to chromosome analysis ("masculine women" and "effeminate men").

Women who model themselves on male executives readily give the impression of being "too aggressive" or "unfeminine". A female manager who wanted to win a colleague over about something in a friendly and polite way reported that her attempt was put down as "petticoat management".

SEX ROLES

The sex role is total. This means it has deeper roots than professional identity. Therefore expectations and performance of job roles are primarily controlled by the cultural pattern, the stereotype personality of the sex dominating the profession. This sex role spillover leads us to expect male nurses to be empathic (cliché: nurse is a woman's job, women are ...), and women in executive positions to be competitive, objectively analytical and rational (cliché: managers are men, men are ...).[3]

Only if these nurses start poisoning their patients and arguing factually and rationally does it become evident that women are not "womanly" of their own accord, but because the labour market only allows them to make use of one side of their potentials. The same pertains to male executives: what should they do with what is called their "feminine" abilities?

Constantly female managers must of necessity perform a balancing act. The high wire has been strung between female identity and the world of men. Since the frame of definition of sex roles entails more than that of occupations, female managers are perceived as "women in jobs" who behave in accordance with their traditional

3   Cf. B. A. Gutek a. B. Morasch (1982): Sex Ratios, Sex Role Spill Over and Sexual Harassment of Women at Work. *Journal of Social Issues* 38: 55-74.

gender role (on the one hand: they should, on the other: they can't). Every female manager is probably aware of the question: "What do you have to say to the problem as a woman?"; and she is surprised when her colleague is asked for his opinion as sales manager. You hardly ever hear the question: "By the way, what do you as a man think about the efficiency of the new office organisation?".

Sex role spillover into the job role leads to a shift of the burden of proof. While men are suitable executives until the opposite comes to light, women have to prove leadership competence first, before it is granted them. However, in effect this handicap is imposed on any new competitor who puts his goods on a market which has been dominated by old-established brand leaders supported by tradition.

MANAGEMENT AS AN ALL-MALE CLUB

To set the right mood, here are a few quotes from women in executive positions:

> "Men usually tend to take on other men. Our division chief, for example, employs people who share his opinions. Or men join and are already intended for a certain position whether they are suitable or not. A woman only makes it to the top by working at it."

> "When I am with them there is a slight, I don't want to say flirtatious, undertone but yes, there is definitely an emotional element there."

> "What I sometimes feel is that men cannot handle women. It would be difficult for the men if they suddenly had a female division chief. They only know women from the home."

> "How you get along with each other depends on several things, and woman-man is simply an additional criterion of reservation which makes it more difficult for men to assess women."

The facts about women and men in executive positions are well-known. More than 90 percent of the higher echelon positions in the economy, public administration and politics are held by men. The higher the position, the less likely it is that a woman is considered for it. In comparable positions, female managers have to wait longer for promotion than their male colleagues.

Management seems to be an all-male club to which women have hardly any access. How can that be explained?

Managing and directing always means acting under great ambiguity. The more responsible the position, the more complex the pertaining tasks, the less clearly defined the rules on how to fulfil these tasks. It is up to the manager to interpret his job description.

In this situation, trust between decision-makers gains importance.[4] "We can rely on each other", the chairman of a multicorporate enterprise once said to his directors with a satisfied smile. The shared agreement of what behaviour one can expect from one another makes it easier to make decisions, as do mutual belief systems, basic assumptions and mentalities. When working together in such thorough coordination, the prerequisites for mutual activities do not have to be redefined over and over again. So next to qualification and competence, the criterion of "fitting in" is at least as important when selecting new executive recruits. Individuals who can be expected to behave "in a similar socially-conscious way" and to adhere to the same unexpressed rules as the existing executives have better chances in management.

Supervisors like to create employees and colleagues in their own image. They literally duplicate themselves in order to encounter confirmation rather than criticism in their work environment. This cloning effect has advantages such as certainty and predictability, but the price to be paid may well be lack of innovation.

One of the most important features of social similarity that has its effect on management is sex.[5] Male managers have to cope with well-tuned habits, tasks or conflicts "among friends", to talk "from man to man", one beer and the matter is settled … Patterns and ritu-

---

4   On the complexity-reducing effect of trust see N. Luhmann (1979): Trust and Power. New York (Wiley); cf. also M. Veith (1988): Frauenkarriere im Management. Einstiegsbarrieren und Diskriminierungsmechanismen. Frankfurt (Campus).

5   R. Kanter (1977): Men and Women of the Corporation. New York (Basic).

155

als to settle rivalry amongst each other are also well-known. It is thus easier to emerge from the competitive situation as the victor.

So men prefer to procure the behaviour of other men. This commodity is familiar, trust and loyalty towards the providers is great, and so it is easier to deal with.

In addition, managers are usually familiar with women in the role of secretaries or partners. These are both complementary relationships. They are not based on similarity but on the difference in behaviour. In these relationships the rules differ from those of symmetrical relationships based on equality of roles.

To a great extent, the attraction of all-male clubs is based on the fact that interaction between men seems to be far less complicated when no women are around. Potentially, sexual competition (often only fantasised) for a woman's favour results in different fields getting mixed up: Are professional or private relationships involved, task-oriented cooperation and rivalry or matters of the heart? When both markets are intertwined, the behaviour of women may, from the perspective of radical market economy, produce an unreasonably high value not usually bestowed them within other "business relationships" (according to many fantasies, at least).

The well-tuned system of attribution of meanings to behaviour amongst men is challenged or becomes ambiguous when women are present. When managers, for instance, signal their mutual good will physically, slap each other on the back, embrace each other etc., this has different implications if the colleague is a woman. Even when you arrange to go out for a drink, all the implications such dates can have between men and women come into play and guarantee an erotic ambiguity which is not always a pleasant experience for the parties concerned.

Consequently it seems only logical (at least it corresponds to the rules of probability) to try and keep the two fields "work" and "private life" carefully separated. Enterprises will only bear the additional costs caused by women in management – the dissolution of the "good old boys' network" and the increased complexity connected with it – if it is experienced as a sound investment. The chances are not so bad, though, because the law of decreasing marginal utility increases women's opportunities. With increasing consumption of a product, the utility and/or the proceeds for a user also increase. At a certain point, however, utility decreases again. Your first beer, for example, satisfies your craving for something wet, the second quenches your thirst, you only drink the third because all the other people around the table are drinking beer, the fourth makes you feel a bit peculiar and the fifth makes you sick … Maybe it would have been better to switch to red wine and then to mineral water after the first beer.

Accordingly, executive positions are reserved for men as long as the proceeds from the synergetic effects of social similarity, simplification and reduction of complexity are considered more profitable than the utility of difference. As soon as it is realised that "more of the same" increases costs and risks for an enterprise because the intuitive potential necessary for development decreases, women will be accepted in executive positions and promoted to fill this market gap.

THE FAMILY AS FITNESS CENTRE

The division of our society into a private and a public domain has different effects on men and women; and this can also be felt in management. The obvious infrastructure for the public sector is prepared in the private sphere, the human environmental prerequisites for its functioning (just as, in turn, the public sphere furnishes the environmental conditions for the private domain). These are co-evolutionary systems that are linked together and mutually limit each other's behavioural and developmental options. A housewife's work, the typical example of "housewifery", is primarily oriented to the basic physiological and emotional needs of the family members (eating, drinking, sleeping, clothing, housing, sexuality, emotions). It requires a great variety of practical organisational abilities and sensitivity. This is where women find their market in our society, here they develop and perfect their abilities. They also cultivate other products since men, in accordance with the distinction between "private" and "public", hardly contribute to the private market or not at all. This is not so much a question of morals or good will, but rather one result of processes of market economy – whether you regret it or not.

In so far as it is performed within the family, housewifery is not paid for with money, but (at best) with "love", "gratitude", "health" and the "well-being of the loved-ones", a "good conscience". That's why women use softener in their washing, do the dusting and perform all the other short-lived, but indispensable chores to maintain order in the home.

This kind of work enjoys only minimal prestige since it is not remunerated.[6] It can only accumulate capital within personal relationships. It is only ever assessed within a certain frame of relationships and solely by direct exchange with the family members.

While monetary payment enables you to save independent of context and to spend what you earned today tomorrow and anywhere you wish (money is a kind of memory), earnings in the direct-exchange business cannot be used in relation to third parties, but can only be claimed within the original relationship. It is tied to the participant's personal memory and the conformity of currencies and accounting. This is why housewifery can result in dependence. Work in a job, on the other hand is paid for with money. The higher the payment, the higher the social prestige, and the easier it thus is to subjugate one's own interests to vocational requirements. Some kind of objectification of "performance" is made, or at least a way of presenting it symbolically that is connected with free convertibility. This creates psychological independence of the actual relationships to the people you are dealing with at work, together with their individual value systems and accounting. Yet this independence is the very thing required in executive positions.

Mostly they are linked to total availability. The distinction between "public" and "private" makes is possible for men to direct their attention to the requirements of the job completely free from domestic duties such as fetching the milk and changing nappies. Generally, division of labour in the "family" firm is highly developed, and for the enterprise the functioning of managers usually depends greatly on the domestic "environmental policy": the manager's physical and psychological regeneration. Thus management jobs are almost always "1 $1/_2$-person jobs".[7] They depend on some-

6 Cf. M. Veith (1990): In: R. Königswieser, U. Froschauer, B. Klipstein, U. Schaub, M. Veith (Eds.): Aschenputtels Portemonnaie. Frauen und Geld. Frankfurt (Campus).

7 E. Beck-Gernsheim (1989): Das halbierte Leben. Frankfurt (Fischer).

one else taking over this supplementary part. If this is not the case, it is inevitable that the rules of management must change.

In the case of so-called "dual career couples"[8] neither the man nor the woman can fall back on the housewifery of a second person. Hence their flexibility decreases and their total availability is challenged (fetching the children from playschool or nursery instead!). Also, international or national transfers necessitate one of the partners coming along (traditionally the woman). If she has a job herself she will be less willing to give it up for her husband's career the more demanding and higher in the hierarchy the position she would have to give up.

All in all, this kind of development leads to more complexity for the organisation of enterprises. These then have to take significantly more environmental factors in the private sphere of their employees into consideration. But changes in management have consequences for the family, too. The more women reach executive positions, the more the traditional forms of division of labour and roles in the family are challenged.

However, this too is a process of evolution. Its dynamics conform neither to decisions and plans, nor to raised index fingers and moral appeals, but to the values and decisions of all participants, to supply and demand which all together form the market for male and female behaviour.

RECIPES

- *Surround yourself only with people like yourself and you are spared thinking about anything new. In this way you can preserve your prejudices against the opposite sex with little effort and decrease the complexity of the situation (of course you won't get all this for free; you forgo the chance of being stimulated by new and unusual ideas and mentalities ...)!*
- *If you want to make use of the opportunities resulting from the differences between men and women you should refrain from sex- specific normativeness. Keep your tacit conviction on how all impor-*

8   T. J. Goodrich, C. Rampage, B. Ellman a. K. Halstead (1991): Feministic Family Therapy. A Casebook. New York (Norton).

tant matters should be handled in check and undertake a journey to a foreign country. If you want to experience the attractions of the local cuisine art on a trip to India, you had better forget your preference for roast pork for a while.

− Take a look at your enterprise and examine which bodies (division chief meetings, board of directors meetings, teams, project groups …) are (almost) exclusively made up of men, which ones include women (if at all …)! What are the advantages and disadvantages of this uniformity?

− Observe how you yourself and others react to good performance and mistakes, to the praise and criticism of men and women in your work environment. What do you have in common, what is different? What are the consequences? What do you want to preserve, what do you want to change?

− To elucidate the differences:

How could you best manage to gain/preserve the conviction that the sex of an employee is not at all relevant within your work environment. How must you behave to achieve this?

How could you best succeed in gaining/preserving the conviction that the sex of an employee is the only important and meaningful factor within your work environment. What must you do to achieve that?

− Imagine that a (good/bad) fairy came tonight and transformed your sex. Tomorrow you would go to work as a man (or woman), if you left your office as a woman (or man) today. What would change for you and for the others in your work environment? Which markets monopolised by men or women respectively would suddenly be open to you or inaccessible from now on?

− Ensure that your scope of action remains as wide as possible.

Don't let the fact that you are a man or a woman entice you to produce behaviour for a (too) narrow market gap. You should neither respect the monopoly claims of the other sex, nor take sex-related commodities for which there is demand off the market. Check whether you are working cost-effectively enough!

9. Learning

"The word 'learning' undoubtedly denotes change of some kind.
To say what kind of change is a delicate matter."

Gregory Bateson[1]

What applies to many a career probably also applies to the career of concepts and slogans used to sell ever changing management fashions: Universal and global usability ensures success. A good example for this is the enthusiasm for learning currently encountered everywhere. Every man and every woman is sentenced to spending all their life at a school desk. Organisations are accused of not doing their homework properly. We are obviously surrounded by private tutors who mean well and know it all and with raised index finger demand learning ability from everyone and everything. Learning is propagated as a value in itself, as a remedy for practically every malaise of our economic system.

It should not be too difficult to agree with the objective of these appeals to increase the flexibility of the economy, its organisations and each individual. The problem of these rather moralising appeals and entreaties is that they are based on relatively naive and slightly antiquated ideas of learning. Above all, however, they overlook the fact that learning and knowledge are not absolute values free of ambivalence. Learning processes do not always have positive effects. Who would query that he has learned an infinite number of unnecessary, sometimes tiresome, occasionally even harmful things in his life? Just think of the improper forehand you acquired in tennis and

---

1   G. Bateson (1964): The Logical Categories of Learning and Communication. In: G. Bateson (1972): Steps to an Ecology of Mind. New York (Ballantine Books) p. 283.

how long it took and how many training hours it cost you to change this once acquired habit of a false motor pattern.

Knowledge can render individuals as well as organisations ignorant and endanger their physical or economic survival; ignorance, on the other hand, can sometimes be a successful strategy.

Thus the questions this chapter is concerned with are: How can we distinguish whether learning is sensible or not? And, if learning turns out to be useful: How do you do it? Or if this is not the case: How can we protect ourselves from learning when we don't want to learn anything at all or when what we learn entails disadvantages for us? How do people and – quite analogously – organisations manage to avoid learning successfully?

People and organisations learn (whether they want to or not). Everything changes. The mystery is not the fact that we learn but the fact that we do not learn: the successful preservation of ignorance, the stability of world views, as well as the stability of organisations and institutions.

Let us begin with a few critical thoughts on language that take us back to the start of our considerations and finally bring our arguments back full circle.

THE STORAGE METAPHOR

Our daily usage of language suggests the idea – as described above in connection with the term information – that in learning we are dealing with the processing of a certain "thing", "material" to be learned or something similar. The danger entailed in such materialistic suggestions is that we deduce teaching and learning methods from them: "Knowledge" is treated as material that can be "drummed into" someone or "collected". Once that has happened you are in command of the "material".

All these images imply a specific inside-outside relationship between the learning system (whether an individual or an organisation) and its environment. Knowledge originally located *outside* (in books, databases or elsewhere) is transported to the *inside* (into a human brain, an organisation, some kind of "store"). What used to be outside before is inside after: You have "got something into your head". In this model, learning can be compared with the activity of an archivist whose creativity is at best limited to the form of cataloguing he uses. Thus knowledge management appears to be an elevated form of stock keeping.

The "material" metaphor also entails the idea that knowledge can be increased in a purely quantitative sense (just as you can add more and more books to a library), and more knowledge is better than less. The increase and decrease of knowledge, however, is subject to different mechanisms from that of material goods. This can be illustrated by the difference between shared knowledge and shared income: If you share your knowledge with another individual you do not have less knowledge than before. Your knowledge has duplicated itself. If you share your income with this individual you only have half left (where knowledge leads to income this difference may cancel itself out).

The storage metaphor for knowledge also suggests that acquiring new knowledge does not have negative consequences for old knowledge. After all, the fact of storing a couple of thousand new books in a library does not adversely affect the quality or readability of old tomes stored there for ages. Under closer consideration, however, these tacit assumptions prove to be false, since the learning done by biological and social systems simply does not function in accordance with the principles of stock keeping.

KNOWLEDGE AND LEARNING AS PRINCIPLES OF EXPLANATION

In order to understand the logic of learning processes, a few principal considerations are required. Let us start with an attempt to define the concept: What are we describing when we talk about knowledge and learning? We use these concepts as observers when we want to explain the behaviour and/or the alteration of the behaviour of a biological or social system, be it a human being or an organisation. We attribute the cause for behaviour that is observable from the outside to some kind of imprecisely defined states or processes within the observed system, i. e. the individual or the organisation: to their "knowledge" or "ignorance". Neither are accessible to direct observation. They are rather hypothetical mechanisms that the observer makes use of to explain the manifestation of the observed patterns of behaviour.

The same applies to the concept of learning. It, too, does not describe the observed behaviour but *explains* it. It attributes the cause for changes in an individual's or an organisation's behaviour over time to changes in their knowledge. An enterprise (an associate) treats his customers friendlier today than a year ago: It (he) has learned to behave in a "customer-oriented" fashion.

Selecting behaviour

Thus knowledge and learning always denote *functions*. Knowledge somehow participates in *selecting behaviour* and learning in *altering* it.

When you base your assumptions on this functional way of looking at things – which seems to be appropriate within the framework of our radical market economy model –, the difference between biological, mental and social structures cancels itself out. When we consider their function for the survival of the respective system knowledge, insight, cognition and life gain a synonymous meaning differing from our colloquial usage: A cognitive system is a system that can act in a certain area of the environment for the purpose of self-preservation. "The process of cognition" – as the neurobiologist Humberto Maturana expresses it – "is real (inductive) action or behaviour in this area. Living systems are cognitive systems and life as a process is a process of cognition."[2]

So biological structures and/or the processes determined by them *are knowledge*. What controls the actual behaviour of an individual, his knowledge, corresponds on a biological level to characteristic networks of nerves, patterns of activity of interacting, mutually activating and deactivating nerve cells.[3] Something analogous can be said about social systems: their structures are cognitive structures, too. An organisation's knowledge manifests itself in its actual day to day functions, the production processes performed anew over

2   H. Maturana (1970): Biology of Cognition, Report 9.0, Biological Computer Laboratory, Department of Electrical Engineering, University of Illinois, Urbana-Champaign/Illinois. Reprinted in: H. R. Maturana, F. J. Varela (1979): Autopoiesis and Cognition. The Realisation of the Living. Boston (Reidel).
3   G. Roth (1995): Das Gehirn und seine Wirklichkeit. Frankfurt (Suhrkamp) pp. 193.

and over again, the repetitive patterns of communication and inter-action among associates and between associates, customers and sup-pliers etc. As long as these factors help to preserve the organisation as an acting unit, this knowledge proves to be appropriate or, in the terminology of evolutionary theory, to "fit". Anyone who survives is fit, his knowledge is good enough. The development of this knowl-edge, its change or non-change, distinction or non-distinction are forms of learning, non-learning, forgetting or unlearning. They can ensure or endanger survival.

The regularities of these processes of learning can be analysed by means of theoretical evolutionary models. At the initial stages of the theory of evolution, survival or extinction of living beings, gen-era or species was regarded as a result of their ability to adapt to a *given* environment. Anyone who dies out, so it seemed, has not learned to adapt to altered environmental conditions in time. This explana-tion for survival and extinction, however, has proved to be too simple. The correlation between a living system and its environment is far more complex: Each living being creates its environment – the market for its behaviour –, it changes or preserves this environment by living, by realising certain modes of behaviour and not others. The same applies to the survival of social systems. Even enterprises create their own environments, their markets, and change them through their behaviour. The development of system and environ-ment is linked, together they bring about a co-evolution. They change each other, determine each other's conditions of survival and adapt to each other.

Who adapts to whom?

Inevitably the focus of attention is drawn to the question of who has to adapt to whom: the individual and/or the organisation to their respective environment or vice versa? Whose structures are more flexible? Are flexibility and learning capability always desirable? It is not always sensible for us to learn and adapt to our environment when this environment could just as easily learn and adapt to us. It is not the firms that – according to expert opinion – have learned to manufacture better state-of-the-art video systems which have been successful on the market, but those whose system found a critical mass of buyers quickest. Apple, who was first to find out how to programme computers to make them easy to use, is struggling to survive because Microsoft made their (originally far more limited) knowledge accessible to a large number of potential competitors. As far as economical success is concerned, it is not always the quality of knowledge that is decisive.

It is therefore advisable to very carefully weigh up and assess what is worth learning and how. To this end it is important to know the mechanisms of non-learning. How do cognitive, i. e. living and social systems get their structures, how do they preserve their identity? How can we learn not to learn in order to assert or preserve the values we consider worth preserving? How can we eliminate these mechanisms of non-learning should it be important for our survival to jettison old knowledge?

Principles

Let us again begin on a theoretical level: Every living system gains information by making distinctions. A selection has to be made from the stream of incoming signals. We have to distinguish between different perceptions, *assess* situations as different or the same, as known or new. Accordingly, behaviour is organised in a familiar or new fashion, differently or the same as before. What the defining attributes of the distinction are depends on the knowledge of the respective living system, its internal structures and processes. In this way former experiences are repeated in dealing with the respective current environment and assumptions about the world confirmed or questioned, prejudices and world views reinforced or modified. Depending on the subtlety of the distinctive criteria, in the course of time, differentiated or undifferentiated *patterns of behaviour* (from the radical market economy view: products) can thus be developed. It is always the environmental reaction to our own behaviour that prompts us to learn or not to learn.

If you want to acquire knowledge you have to act, and if you want to impart knowledge you have to give behavioural instructions. If you want to teach someone what a cake is and what it tastes like you should provide him with a recipe. You not only have to tell him what to do to make a cake (how to mix which ingredients in which sequence and what external influences they have to be exposed to), you also have to tempt him somehow to bake and eat this cake. This is the only way to enable your apprentice to experience what is typical about a cake: its smell, taste, the ingredients, how it is made etc.

The fact that cognition and behaviour are a unity is proved when recipes are put into use.

Learning, forgetting and unlearning are alterations of distinctions. Non-learning, on the other hand, is the preservation of existing distinctions. This necessitates repetition of the behaviour that led to these distinctions and avoidance of behaviour that might lead to new distinctions.

The development of a living system in interaction with its environment is a history of structural changes, i. e. alterations of distinctions. Environmental events work as perturbations, they do not fit the patterns of distinction used so far. Old distinctions have to be abolished and new ones made. Environmental events that do not work as a perturbation do not lead to any structural change of the system, i. e. they have no value as information and no learning effect.

Thus knowledge and learning are opposites. Where knowledge is preserved, learning is prevented. Therefore knowledge cannot simply be increased like the size of a cake: Learning destroys knowledge by preventing old distinctions to continue to be made. In order to promote learning, you have to provide perturbations and question old truths.

The prevention of learning

Let us now deal with the strategies of non-learning in the sense of the positive force of negative thinking: If it is possible to experience the environment as unchanged, the given repertoire of behaviour and differentiation is sufficient to react to all contingencies. Whatever happens, it has all happened before. Every challenge caused by environmental events is met with the answer: That's the way it's always been, we've always done it like that. Nothing new happens in interaction between system and environment, nothing perturbs it, there is no need to learn anything.

There are several possibilities of assuring these experiences of a constant world: The first is to ensure stability of your own environment by your own actions. The second possibility is to ensure a stable perception of the environment by systematically excluding information.

The first method is quite widespread: It explains why some people primarily surround themselves with individuals who neither do nor say anything unpredictable or unforeseeable and only read newspapers propagating their own views. This can be seen as prophylaxis against disturbances, a strategy for chronicity of one's own thinking – if assessed negatively – and a strategy to preserve one's own identity – if assessed positively.

The second method for not letting yourself be irritated by a changed environment is simply not to perceive it as new and to exclude changes as unthinkable even for the future. After all, everyone decides for himself what is and is not new for him, what he considers different and what is not different. If you only take note of information that confirms your own background, neither conflicts nor the need for learning or change develop. If what is assumed to be new is not treated as new, then the structure which is most languid will assert itself. The formula might read like this: Obstinacy can prevent you from changing your ways too quickly.

So from the perspective of the external observer we can establish that confirmation of knowledge, whether brought about actively or experienced passively – this can never be separated distinctly –, is the best prerequisite for successful non-learning.[4] Reduced to a handy formula: Knowledge gives you learning problems, success makes you educationally subnormal. If you make no mistakes now, nor fear making any in the future – you have no reason to learn. Nobody repairs cars that work. No change without impetus.

This might be the reason why many people learn less and less the older they get: They simply know enough to get on in life without too much trouble. The same applies, of course, to long-standing organisations and institutions such as schools. Schools are a typical example for the fact that organisations in which you learn are not necessarily learning organisations. On the contrary: there are probably few organisations with as many learning problems as schools.

4   For greater detail see F. B. Simon (1997): Die Kunst, nicht zu lernen. Und andere Paradoxien aus Psychotherapie, Management, Politik … Heidelberg (Carl-Auer)

As there is a constant stream of new pupils, teachers as well as schools can reckon with environments that remain constant. They function on the principle of an instantaneous water heater. Illiterates are pushed in on one side, and on the other sufficiently civilised citizens come out who have (more or less) learnt reading, writing and arithmetic, and have generally acquired the necessary social techniques to enable them to participate in the usual party games. Even instantaneous water heaters only fur up so successfully because there is a continuous supply of new water. As far as school is concerned, it seems neither necessary nor economically sensible to come up with new ideas. Why launch a new product when the old one still sells well?

Someone who knows that he knows and knows that his knowledge possibly makes him ignorant can lose his learning problems. He can inquisitively question his old distinctions and routines in order to unlearn them. When an individual or an organisation manages to examine the usefulness of their daily recurring behavioural patterns and functional patterns critically, they can choose whether to initiate alternative patterns of behaviour, interaction and communication and thus change themselves and their environment, or to carry on doing everything the same way as before.

If we look at the plain facts, it should be obvious that there are no clear and unequivocal preferences for learning or not learning. Both involve risks and need to be assessed ambivalently. We always have to pay the price, whether we learn or not. One thing should be clear, however: functional ignorance is not simply God-given, it has to be learned. Everyone should know that.

RECIPES

- *Don't begrudge yourself (alone or even better with the other participants) the role of author of a cookery book: Collect recipes. If you regard organisations as a kind of stew, the ingredients are the modes of behaviour of the participating chefs. Try to describe what is being done day by day. Who does what when, in which sequence and what are the others doing then? What is the result? Is it enjoyable, agreeable or does it make you sick? How do the people that have to digest it all react? When these recipes are used, do they lead to the develop-*

ment of food for which there is a market? In other, somewhat less poetic words: What are the patterns of interaction and communication of the organisational units whose learning, forgetting and unlearning is involved? These units of learning can be a single associate – you, for instance –, a division, a sector, an enterprise. Recipes describe process patterns, the processes through which an organisation evolves, i. e. the actual knowledge of the organisation. Try at first to describe without assessing.

In a second step, assess how the cost-benefit analysis of the respective behaviour turns out for the involved units (different individual associates, different organisational units, total organisation). Who gains and who loses what through which change? How do the various environments (e. g. suppliers, customers, the public) react to these patterns or rather to what can be observed from the outside?

– *Employ these phases for reflection to direct attention to very concrete processes whenever you have the feeling that you and/or your organisation have concocted something hard to digest, detrimental or even poisonous. Even if you have the impression that your competitors are better cooks, you should squeeze in phases for reflection. However, in this case you should also collect competitors' recipes. Even when there is no particular reason for doing so, you should regularly check whether your recipes are still up-to-date, whether some ingredients should be omitted or new ones added.*

– *Use your sense of feasibility when reflecting on long-established processes and planning. Always go through both sides of the distinction when assessing possible alternatives: If there is no change in the processes, what kind of consequences will this have in the future, and when? Would their evaluation be positive or negative? Would they in all probability (the future cannot be foreseen) rather increase or decrease the probability of survival? What kind of unintentional side effects would there be if you change or refrain from changing something. As a trial, question your favourite truths. Carry out thought experiments – that is the only way to learn (invent) what no one yet knows!*

– *Use the creative potential of group processes. One of their creative principles is that no one can control this process. This makes it more difficult for the participants to swim in their "own sauce" (if we stick to kitchen metaphors). This means that the tendency of human thinking to construct consistent and self-confirming world views is inevitably disturbed, knowledge is questioned, learning made possible.*

- *Invent ideas together with others and don't let yourself be restricted by individual participants' sense of reality (reality itself makes sure that it is not forgotten – but who says it might not adapt to crazy ideas?). Don't begrudge yourself a mutual portion of megalomania! We owe everything great to megalomania.*

10. Postscript – about this book

"A clash of doctrines is not a disaster, it is an opportunity."
Alfred N. Whitehead[1]

*"In addition to all the engineering and business courses,
I also studied four years of psychology and abnormal psychology
at Lehigh. I'm not being facetious when I say that
these were probably the most valuable courses
of my college career. It makes for a bad pun, but it's true:
I've applied more of those courses in dealing
with the nuts I've met in the corporate world
than all the engineering courses
in dealing with the nuts (and bolts) of automobiles."*
Lee Iacocca[2]

It is not often that a psychiatrist and a group of management consultants write a book together. It seems that two fields have come together, that don't really have anything to do with one another. And yet this combination is actually quite logical and consistent.

The objective of management consultation is to organise and structure the professional interaction of human beings in a rational manner. How they feel, think and act structures the rules of human systems – the rules of an enterprise, for instance. Psychiatrists deal with the question of how madness, i. e. the disorganisation of thinking, feeling and acting, develops. But human thinking, feeling and

---

1   A. N. Whitehead (1925): Science and the Modern World. New York (Free Press), 1967, p. 186.
2   L. Iacocca, W. Novak (1984): Iacocca. An Autobiography. Toronto/New York (Bantam Books), p. 22.

acting is controlled – here the circuit is closed – by the rules of inter-personal communication and interaction (primarily the rules of a relationship between two people or in a family, but also in an enterprise). While management consultants direct their attention to the functioning, generation and maintenance of order, the psychiatrist studies the mechanisms of the dissolution of order, the development of chaos. From the perspective of the theory of living systems, however, both sides belong together. They are the two sides of the same coin.

It is certainly no coincidence that the clash of doctrines in the form of longstanding cooperation between the specialist for insanity and the specialists for reality has led to the development of a model in which the differences between psychology and economy are counterbalanced. Economy, so they say, is 80 percent psychology – but from the point of view of radical market economy, psychology proves to be 100 percent economy.

Nevertheless, you need to be wary of this book or rather of the models presented therein. They, too, are a theoretical construct enabling us to grasp the processes of life, and these theories will long be a thing of the past whilst frogs continue to exist. For this reason we emphasise once again in all modesty the claims of our model of a radical market economy. It is not about truth, but about usefulness, about reducing complexity, about a map to make orientation easier in the confusing, often chaotic and seemingly unfathomable everyday life of an enterprise – and nothing else (but that is really quite a lot …)!

About the Authors

Fritz B. Simon, M. D., Professor for Management and Organisation, Economics Faculty of the University of Witten/Herdecke, Germany. Systemic organisation consultant, psychiatrist, psychoanalyst and systemic family therapist. Managing partner of Management Zentrum Witten GmbH and Simon, Weber and Friends, Systemic Organisation Consultation GmbH. From 1994 to 2001, vice president of the European Family Therapy Association (EFTA), vice president of the German-Chinese Academy for Psychotherapy. Main focus of work: organisation, communication and conflict research and consultation, coaching. Teaching and consultation in various European countries, the United States and China. Author and/or editor of approx. 200 scientific articles and 17 books, which have been translated into 10 languages.

C/O/N/E/C/T/A Author Group:

Eva Dachenhausen, Organisational consultant and trainer. Group dynamicist (LT, LB in the ÖGGO), systemic family therapist, supervisor, coach. Responsible for the training committee of the ÖGGO. Served as managing partner of C/O/N/E/C/T/A for many years.

Gerardo Drossos, PhD. Consultant and trainer. Studied sociology and economics in Vienna; trained in systemic organisations counselling in Vienna and Palo Alto. Works for major Austrian daily paper; personnel manager, chief trainer and head of the management development unit of a large Austrian bank. Since 1992, consultant for the Austrian Association of Savings Banks. Executive shareholder of C/O/N/E/C/T/A.

Alfred Janes, PhD., Professor. Consultant and coach. Studied economic engineering and sociology at the University of Graz; trained in systemic organisational consulting at the Institute for Family Therapy, Heidelberg. Assistant professor at the Department of Labour and Operations Science at the Technical University of Vienna, teaches labour science, organisation and group dynamics. Trainer for group dynamics trainers and training consultant for systemic organisational consulting at the Austrian Society for Group Dynamics and Organisation Counselling (ÖGGO); teaching assignments at the Institute for Interdisciplinary Research and Continued Training of the Universities of Klagenfurt, Vienna, Innsbruck and Graz (iff); since 1995, full professor of Industrial Operations and Change Management at the Technical University of Graz. Managing partner of C/O/N/E/C/T/A since 1986.

Ingrid Kreuzer, PhD. Consultant and coach. Studied pedagogy, philosophy and psychology at the University of Vienna; trained in systemic organisational consulting at DGSD eV, Ludwigshafen, Germany. Management position in a major financial services company in the field of human resources development and management development. Training consultant at the ÖGGO. Managing partner of C/O/N/E/C/T/A since 1991.

Karl Prammer, PhD. Consultant and trainer. Studied mechanical engineering with a focus on operations science at the Technical University of Vienna; lectures on ethnology at the University of Vienna, trained in systemic organisational consulting at the Institute for Family Therapy, Heidelberg. Work with research society for the advancement of innovations; assistant professor at the Department of Labour and Operations Science, teaches and does research in labour science, organiser of free-lance labour scientists, expert advisor, management trainer and process consultant work on research project for a major international IT corporation in the United States; head of the Organisation and Information division of a Swiss insurance company in Zurich. Associated member of ÖGGO; since 1987, lecturer at the International Summer Academy of Ergonomics in Györ, Hungary; since 1992, executive shareholder, advisor and trainer with C/O/N/E/C/T/A; since 1995, teaching assignments at the iff.

Herbert Schober, M.A. Consultant and trainer. Master craftsman and engineer in electrical engineering; studied sociology and economics at the Vienna University of Economics; trained in systemic organisational consulting, group dynamics and socio-psychology. Management and strategy development in a financial services company, 1976 co-founder of C/O/N/E/C/T/A. Lecturer at the University of Klagenfurt, trainer of trainers and training consultant for ÖGGO; since 1972, work as a consultant; since 1976, executive shareholder of C/O/N/E/C/T/A.

Michael Schulte-Derne, PhD. Consultant and coach. Studied sociology and economics at the Vienna University of Economics; trained in systemic organisational consulting at the Institute for Family Therapy, Heidelberg. Manager in retailing, service and research. Teaching assignments at the iff. Member of the Austrian Study Society for Cybernetics. Training consultant for systemic organisation counselling at the ÖGGO. Managing partner of C/O/N/E/C/T/A since 1988.

Monika Veith, PhD. Consultant and coach. Studied sociology and economics at the Vienna University of Economics; post-graduate studies in sociology; trained in group dynamics, systems theory, systemic counselling, body and energy work. Product manager with a multinational corporation, managing director of an Austrian consulting company. Member of the ÖGGO. Managing partner of C/O/N/E/C/T/A since 1991.

Helga Weule, PhD. Trainer and consultant. Undergraduate and doctoral studies at the University of Vienna. Training as group dynamics coach and trainer of trainers and consultant for the ÖGGO. Training and continuing education in gestalt analysis, bioenergetic analysis and systemic family therapy. Member of TEMPUS (Time deceleration society). Since 1994, adjunct instructor at the Institute of Organisation Research at the University of Linz. In 2000, co-founded the Institute for Consciousness Strategies in Bad Tölz. 1984–1993, managing partner of C/O/N/E/C/T/A.